THOMAS MORE

THOMAS MORE

The Search for the Inner Man

❖ ❖ ❖ ❖ ❖ ❖ ❖ ❖ ❖

LOUIS L. MARTZ

Yale University Press ❖ New Haven & London

Previously published portions of the book are reproduced by permission as follows: ch. 1 (revised), from *Miscellanea Moreana*, ed. Murphy, Gibaud, & Di Cesare, © 1989, Center for Medieval and Early Renaissance Studies, State University of New York at Binghamton; materials in ch. 2 and ch. 3, from *Moreana*, No. 62 (1979) and Nos. 15–16 (1967); materials in ch. 4, from *Thought*, 52 (1977), 300–318, © 1977 by Fordham University Press.

Published with assistance from the Louis Effingham deForest Memorial Fund.

Designed by Richard Hendel.
Set in Aldus type by
G & S Typesetters, Austin, Texas.
Printed in the United States of America by Book Crafters, Chelsea, Michigan.

Library of Congress Cataloging-in-Publication Data
Martz, Louis Lohr.
Thomas More : the search for the inner man / Louis L. Martz.
    p.   cm.
Includes bibliographical references.
ISBN 0–300–04784–3 (alk. paper)
1. More, Thomas, Sir, Saint, 1478–1535—Criticism and interpretation.   I. Title.
PR2322.M35   1990
942.05′2′092—dc20   90–31140
[B]   CIP

The paper in this book meets the guidelines for permanence and durability of the Committee on Production Guidelines for Book Longevity of the Council on Library Resources.

10 9 8 7 6 5 4 3 2 1

To the Memory of

Richard S. Sylvester

Contents

Illustrations

Acknowledgments

Whatever insights this book may contain are constantly indebted to the community of editors who for thirty years have worked together to create the Yale Edition of More's works. My greatest debt is due to the friend, colleague, and former student to whom this book is dedicated.

I wish also to thank the following for their advice in preparing this volume: Ellen Graham, for her suggestion that the original essays should be developed into a book, with quotations modernized; the anonymous reader for the Yale Press, who offered essential suggestions for revision; Caroline Murphy, for perceptive editing; and Clarence Miller, for his careful reading of the manuscript, with many creative suggestions. I am grateful to Jane Roberts, Curator of the Print Room in the Royal Library, Windsor Castle, for permission to examine the original drawings of More by Holbein, and to reproduce them here; to the Öffentliche Kunstsammlung, Basel, for permission to reproduce the Holbein drawing of More's family; to Lord St. Oswald for permission to reproduce the Lockey version of the Holbein family group, to the Royal Academy of Arts for providing a photograph of this painting, and to Brian Allen, of The Paul Mellon Centre for Studies in British Art, for assistance in acquiring this photograph.

L. L. M.

❖ ❖ ❖ ❖ ❖ ❖ ❖ ❖ ❖

The Search for the Inner Man

Most of us, I imagine, have held in our minds an image of Thomas More shaped directly or indirectly by the classic biography by R. W. Chambers, or influenced by the similar figure created by Robert Bolt in *A Man for All Seasons:* the image of a man humane, wise, and witty, honest in his work as judge and lawyer, devoted to and loved by his family and friends, but underneath all this, a man of conscience so strong that he would die rather than bend his beliefs to suit the demands of a ruthless tyranny.

But this image has recently become a matter of severe debate, mainly because of the studies of G. R. Elton and the massive new biography of More by Richard Marius.[1] The debate has extended far beyond the walls of academe, until it has come to influence a recent production of *A Man for All Seasons.* This is clear from an interview in the *New York Times* with Philip Bosco, who played the role of More in the New York production of 1987. In 1961 Bosco was an understudy for the roles of Henry VIII and Norfolk in Paul Scofield's production of the play. But now he questions the interpretation of More that he watched so intently from the wings twenty-five years ago: "Mr. Bosco knows," we read in the *Times,* "through rehearsal talk about the play's period, that Mr. Bolt's image of Sir Thomas More is conspicuously lacking warts. He also knows that the figure who was to achieve sainthood was immoderately proud of his high position in the realm and fierce, indeed, bloodthirsty on the subject of heretics."[2]

"Rehearsal talk" has apparently been affected by the new biography, for this view of More's treatment of heretics, disseminated long ago by John Foxe's *Book of Martyrs,* and laid to rest for a while by modern scholars, is vehemently resurrected by Marius as a basic theme: "His fury at the Protestant heretics . . . has a touch of hysteria about it, and although we may exonerate him from old charges that he tied heretics to a tree in his yard at Chelsea and beat them, he was if anything inclined to an even greater savagery against them, for he cried for them to be burned alive, and he rejoiced when some of them went to the fire. This fury was not a bizarre lapse in an otherwise noble character; it was almost the essence of the man" (p. xxiv). Clearly this view goes far beyond the recognition of certain blemishes in the complexion: it offers a radical alteration in our image of the man.

It is true that More frequently declared that those convicted of heresy were "well and worthily burned," but these words seem to me to represent a judge's grim approval of the well-deserved punishment of a criminal who has committed what More calls the worst of crimes—the crime of leading other souls to eternal perdition. "And for heretics as they be," says More, "the clergy doth denounce them. And as they be well worthy, the temporality doth burn them. And after the fire of Smithfield, hell doth receive them, where the wretches burn forever."[3] In passages such as this I do not hear a note of hysteria or rejoicing, but rather a tone of fearsome warning and somber satisfaction at finding justice done.

More did pursue rigorously those suspected of heresy; he questioned them, according to his own account, with a mixture of severity and charity, and he turned them over to the religious authorities for trial when he found his suspicions warranted. This is what his duty required under the statutes of the realm, and it was certainly a duty that More willingly performed, as he makes clear in his *Apology*. Here, for example, is how he describes the way in which he apprehended Thomas Philips "of London leatherseller":[4]

> Whom when I was chancellor, upon certain things that I
> found out by [i.e., concerning] him, by the examination of
> divers heretics whom I had spoken with, upon the occasion

of the heretics' forboden [i.e., forbidden] books, I sent for; and when I had spoken with him, and honestly entreated him one day or twain in mine house, and labored about his amendment in as hearty loving manner as I could: when I perceived finally the person such that I could find no truth, neither in his word nor his oath, and saw the likelihed that he was in the setting forth of such heresies closely [i.e., secretly], a man meet and likely to do many folk much harm: I by indenture delivered him to his ordinary [i.e., to the ecclesiastical authority]. [*CW*, 9 : 126]

Prosecution of heretics increased around 1529, the year More became Lord Chancellor, because the instances of heresy were multiplying rapidly. At the same time Henry VIII—frustrated over his prospects for a divorce and anxious to have a male heir, especially one by Anne Boleyn—was beginning to listen sympathetically to certain aspects of heretical thought. Clerics who supported the divorce, such as John Stokesley, could demonstrate their underlying orthodoxy by hunting out heretical books and people. Meanwhile, those who opposed the divorce, such as Thomas More and Cuthbert Tunstall, could use the same means to remind Henry of the dangers of heresy and of the enmity Henry himself had displayed toward Martin Luther in his *Assertio septem sacramentorum*—a book that More constantly and shrewdly brings to the king's attention.

The pursuit of heretics continued after More's resignation and after his death, though usually for different reasons. The basic cause was still religious, but the charge now was typically treason—that is, refusing to accept Henry's supremacy over the church. We are told that in the five years following April 1535 (three months before More's execution) Thomas Cromwell engaged in vigorous personal prosecution of those suspected of continuing to support the papacy, and during those five years "something like sixty-five" people suffered the "horrible execution" decreed for treason.[5] This figure, of course, does not include the thirteen or fourteen Anabaptists condemned in May 1535 or the Nun of Kent and her five followers, condemned a year earlier, nor does it include the nearly two hundred who were executed for their part in the northern uprisings. By contrast, More was "personally involved" in prosecuting only three out of the six cases of heresy in all of England that led to burning during the three years of his chancellorship.[6]

My point is not to show that one party was worse than another. No doubt More and his party—the faction working behind the scenes to prevent the divorce—would have been equally ruthless had they been able to summon equal power. My point is simply that the political procedures of the age were cruel and ruthless on either side; it is therefore difficult to argue that Thomas More's prosecution of those he suspected of heresy was any more severe than Thomas Cromwell's prosecution of those he suspected of treason. For both it was a grim matter of quelling what they, for different reasons, saw as seditious. Let us lay aside, then, this ancient and unfounded charge against More.

I should like to try another approach, implicit in the visual images of More and his family presented by Hans Holbein. Consider first the pen-and-ink drawing preserved in the museum at Basel and presented by More to Erasmus as a token of friendship (figure 1). Let me first introduce the characters. Starting from the left, we see More's daughter Elizabeth; next to her, More's foster-daughter, Margaret Giggs, leaning over to point out a place in a book to More's father, Judge John More; seated next, Thomas More, aged fifty; in between Sir John and Sir Thomas, the small figure of the young lady destined to carry on the male line: More's ward, Anne Cresacre, soon to marry More's son John, standing next to his father. The burly figure facing us by the doorway is More's fool, Henry Patenson. Be-

FIGURE 1.
Hans Holbein the Younger, *Sir Thomas More and His Family*,
Öffentliche Kunstsammlung, Kupferstichkabinett, Basel.

low him, seated, is More's daughter Cecily, with a rosary in her left hand. Prominent in the right foreground is More's favorite child, Margaret Roper, and at the far right, More's second wife, Dame Alice, significantly kneeling at a prie-dieu, with her eyes cast down upon an open book which we assume must be a prayer book of some kind. The cross on the chain before the book adds to the devotional atmosphere. And now we note that all the books that the characters are holding are quite small and seem to be prayer books. Larger books are lying on the floor and on the shelf by the window, temporarily laid aside, it would seem. Perhaps Margaret Giggs is pointing out the place in the prayer book for a service that is about to begin.

But if so, why is Sir Thomas not kneeling to lead the service, as his wife is kneeling? I think he is about to do so. Near More's right foot is a low footstool, which from an aesthetic point of view serves neatly to center and focus the scene. But what purpose might it serve in the scene's dramatic moment? Is More about to leave his seat, kneel upon the stool, and lead a service of devotion? Note, too, the angle of the stool's placement: it is in line with the direction in which some of the figures are gazing—toward the viewer's right. What are they gazing at? What would More, kneeling on the footstool so centrally placed, look at as he leads the service? Something is beyond the drawing that we cannot see: perhaps a crucifix, a shrine, or a painting. In any case it seems beyond doubt that the drawing presents the group as a devotional service is about to begin.

Now there are at Windsor Castle two drawings of More by Holbein, one of which is closely allied to the image of More in this drawing of the devotional group, while the other is the prototype of the famous oil portrait now in the Frick Collection. We need to compare these closely. The prototype of the Frick painting (figure 2) presents an image of firm control. The large black hat dominates the face, set down low upon the brow, and the hair, cut short, is firmly restrained within the hat. The facial expression is resolute, suitable to a lawyer, judge, royal counsellor, and statesman. The furred gown (hiding the hair shirt) shows his high estate, giving further support to the firm countenance. Experts in art much prefer this drawing to the other. After all, it is more thoroughly done, and the hair and robe are colored. The other Windsor drawing, a lightly tinted sketch (figure 3), has been called feebler, less skillfully done.[7] It may be weaker, in some sense, but is it less skillful? It is in every way more relaxed, more open: the hat is softer and reveals more of the forehead, while the long hair flows out freely from beneath it on either side. We see the face of a man unguarded, open, vulnerable, seeking, devotional in his mood. Even the lack of color in the robe adds to this effect, for we cannot see this man's worldly status: it is of no importance. Perhaps we tend to underrate the skill of this sketch because we are so accustomed to the More of the Frick portrait, with its stern, strong, formidable guise. Holbein, in the devotional drawing of More, seems to have given us a rare glimpse of the unguarded More, the inner man seeking the strength of his faith to support him. Here is the sensitive, humane, and humanist More who loves his Latin and his Greek, also the More who in his youth said his prayers at the Charterhouse, the More who might have been a churchman. He chose to follow the career of lawyer, judge, and statesman represented by the facial expression and the robe and regalia found in the Frick portrait. But underneath lies the sensitive, seeking spirit of the religious devotee, the humanist, the lover of ancient languages.

It is the humanist scholar that we find in the great tempera portrait of the family by Holbein, now destroyed, but extant to some degree in the apparently faithful replica made by Rowland Lockey around 1593 and now housed at Nostell Priory (figure 4).[8] The devotional atmosphere of the drawing is here removed.

FIGURE 2.
Hans Holbein the Younger, *Sir Thomas More*,
Windsor Castle, Royal Library (RL 12268).

FIGURE 3.
Hans Holbein the Younger, *Sir Thomas More*,
Windsor Castle, Royal Library (RL 12225).

FIGURE 4.
Rowland Lockey, after Hans Holbein the Younger,
Sir Thomas More and His Family, Nostell Priory.

Dame Alice, in accordance with a note written by Holbein on
the Basel sketch, is now sitting, not kneeling. Cecily's rosary is
gone. The footstool is gone. Most of the books visible are now
much larger, and some of them can be identified. Elizabeth has
under her right arm a book labeled as Seneca's Epistles, while
the book on Margaret Roper's lap is open to a readable page in
the fourth act of Seneca's *Oedipus*. One of the books on the
sideboard is labeled as Boethius's *Consolation of Philosophy*.
Margaret Giggs has changed places with Elizabeth, and one may
see a certain propriety in the fact that no one is pointing out the
place in a classical book to Sir John, who did not at all approve of
his son's attraction to the life of humanist learning. A figure has
been added—More's secretary, leaning in the doorway. The
whole scene is now that of More's little "Academy," where the
women were able to read Latin as well as the men. It is the atmosphere More evokes in a delightful letter that he wrote to his
children from court in 1521. The letter is in Latin, though some
of the children addressed were only twelve or thirteen: if they
could not read Latin easily by then there was no hope for them.
Nevertheless, I will quote in translation:

> Thomas More to his Whole School Greeting.
>   See what a compendious salutation I have found, to save
> both time and paper, which would otherwise have been
> wasted in listing the names of each one of you in salutation,
> and my labor would have been to no purpose, since, though
> each of you is dear to me by some special title, of which I
> could have omitted none in an ingratiating salutation, no
> one is dearer to me by any title than each of you by that of
> scholar. . . . But I think you have no longer any need of
> Master Nicholas, since you have learned whatever he had to
> teach you about astronomy. I hear you are so far advanced
> in that science that you can not only point out the polar star

or the dog star, or any of the ordinary stars, but are able also . . . to distinguish the sun from the moon! Onward then in that new and admirable science by which you ascend to the stars! But while you gaze on them assiduously, consider that this holy time of Lent warns you, and that beautiful and holy poem of Boethius keeps singing in your ears, teaching you to raise your mind also to heaven, lest the soul look downwards to the earth, after the manner of brutes, while the body is raised aloft.

Farewell, all my dearest.

From Court, the 23rd March.[9]

We will never understand More unless we give full weight to the love of humanist learning and the love of family shown in this letter and in the Nostell portrait. What then shall we make of his youthful sojourn with the monks of the Charterhouse, of the hair shirt, and of the practice of whipping the flesh reported by William Roper? It has been argued that these ascetic practices indicate More's longing for the life of a medieval monk and his sense of guilt because sexual desire had led him to marry and lead a life in the world.[10] But such severities could serve also to mortify the pride of worldly place as More advanced in the king's service, and we know for a fact that More, as his prosperity increased, wrote a long meditation on the seven deadly sins, showing, as St. Bernard and many others had shown, that the primary sin, the root of all the others, was pride.[11]

We need to examine closely the events of More's early life to see what evidence there is to support the oft-repeated view that More longed for the monastic life. Nicholas Harpsfield, following Roper and family tradition, probably gives the best account. From it we gather that from around 1500 to 1504, when he was twenty-two to twenty-six years old, More was attempting to pursue simultaneously at least four different interests: practice

in the law, study of Greek, study of theology, and religious devotion. After his boyhood training in the household of Archbishop Morton, later Cardinal Morton (strongly praised in the
Utopia), More was sent at Morton's urging to Oxford.

> This Cardinal then that had raised both to himself and
> others such an expectation to this child, being now more
> and more careful to have him well trained up, that his
> goodly bud might be a fair flower, and at length bring forth
> such fruit as he and the others expected and looked for,
> thought it best he should be sent to the University of Ox-
> ford, and so he was; where, for the short time of his abode
> (being not fully two years) and for his age, he wonderfully
> profited in the knowledge of the Latin and Greek tongues;
> where, if he had settled and fixed himself, and had run his
> full race in the study of the liberal sciences and divinity, I
> trow he would have been the singular and the only spectacle
> of this our time for learning.[12]

And surely something in this line is what Morton would have
had in mind when he recommended Oxford for the boy: a distinguished career as a scholarly man of the Church, leading perhaps to political involvement such as Morton himself had known.

More's father had quite different ideas, as Harpsfield goes on
to tell:

> But his father minded that he should tread after his steps,
> and settle his whole mind and study upon the laws of the
> Realm. And so being plucked from the universities of stud-
> ies and learnings, he was set to the studies of the laws only
> of this Realm. [p. 12]

Although More pursued his legal studies vigorously, nevertheless, Harpsfield adds,

he cut off from the study of the law much time, which he employed to his former studies that he used in Oxford; and especially to the reading of St. Augustine *de Civitate Dei*, which though it be a book very hard for a well learned man to understand . . . yet did Master More, being so young, being so distracted also and occupied in the study of the common laws, openly read [i.e., give lectures on] in the Church of St. Laurence in London the books of the said St. Augustine *de Civitate Dei*, to his no small commendation, and to the great admiration of all his audience. His lesson [i.e., his lecturing] was frequented and honored with the presence and resort, as well of that well learned and great cunning man, Master Grocyn (with whom and with Master Thomas Lupset[13] he learned the Greek tongue) as also with the chief and best learned men of the City of London. [pp. 13–14]

At the same time he was not only pursuing his career in law but was also active as a Burgess of Parliament, incurring the enmity of Henry VII in 1504 by his opposition to a subsidy, and he was also performing devotions with the monks of the Charterhouse.

And all this while was he unmarried, and seemed to be in some doubt and deliberation with himself what kind and trade of life he should enter, to follow and pursue all his long life after. Surely it seemeth by some apparent conjectures that he was sometime somewhat propense and inclined either to be a priest, or to take some monastical and solitary life [note the alternative that Harpsfield here allows]; for he continued after his foresaid reading four years and more full virtuously and religiously in great devotion and prayer with the monks of the Charterhouse of London, without any manner of profession or vow [and here again

Harpsfield allows for an alternative set of choices], either to see and prove whether he could frame himself to that kind of life, or at least for a time to sequester himself from all temporal and worldly exercises. [p. 17]

These devotions at the Charterhouse must have gone on concurrently with his work as a lawyer, for there is no evidence at all that he gave up his legal profession to enter upon a concentrated four-year retreat. Whether or not he actually lived in the Charterhouse remains uncertain; in any case, with More's habit of early rising, he could have performed his devotions for several hours in the very early morning, attended to his legal business for most of the day, and returned to the Charterhouse for further devotions in the evening. As Harpsfield suggests at the end of the passage just quoted, it appears that More used the Charterhouse as a place for meditation and prayer concerning his vocation, to perform what were later called "exercises of election"—spiritual exercises performed in order to see if he would follow a religious or a secular career. But his choice of the Charterhouse as the place to pursue these meditations does not necessarily indicate (as Harpsfield recognized) a tendency toward the monastic life.[14] Everything else we know of More's activity during these early years indicates that he is tending toward a scholarly life in the world, such as his good friends Colet, Grocyn, Linacre, and Erasmus were pursuing—a career in orders that would satisfy his religious instinct as well as his love of scholarship and literature, a career that might well lead to high office in the church and important influence in the affairs of state. We might think of this young More as a future Bishop of London, Archbishop of York, or Archbishop of Canterbury—all positions in which his legal training would have been of great advantage. We may well believe that More could have reached such high office. It seems more likely that this sort

of career was in More's mind than the monastic life. Harpsfield
and others, I think, have put far too much weight upon two
later utterances of More in moments of great stress.

> Himself said also afterward, when his daughter Margaret
> Roper . . . escaped against all expectation . . . of a most
> dangerous sickness, that if she had died, he would never
> have intermeddled with any worldly affairs after. Further-
> more, being prisoner in the Tower, he told his said daughter
> that his short penning and shutting up did little grieve him;
> for if it had not been for respect [i.e., consideration] of his
> wife and children, he had voluntarily long ere that time
> shut himself in as narrow or narrower a room than that
> was. [pp. 17–18]

But these are later thoughts, twenty-five or thirty years later,
and the last is a hypothetical thought in a time of complete political failure.[15] They bear little weight when we are considering
the options of this gifted young man, protégé and admirer of
Cardinal Morton, a young man whose studies in law, language,
and divinity could well combine in distinguished service for the
church in the active life. But More, after four years of hesitation
and meditation, chose to marry and to stay with the law. Why
did he do so? I think it was not only because he suffered from
sexual desire, though no doubt this played a part in his decision.
It seems likely that he wished to raise a family and continue his
father's line, in accordance with the duty of an elder son. And
this was also, we certainly may believe, the vehement desire of
the strong-minded father whom he loved and honored. The re-
port of Erasmus that More gave up the priesthood because he
wanted a wife must be taken in the known context of his father's very strong pressures in the secular direction and More's
sense of family duty.[16]

The decision to pursue a career in the law instead of a career in the church may have important implications for More's later writings and death. As he watched one bishop after another, and in the end even Warham and Tunstall, bow to the pressures of the king, what might the inner man have felt? Had I been there in a post of churchly power, he may have asked himself, could I perhaps have helped to turn affairs another way? We do not know what would have happened if a strong archbishop had led the opposition to Henry. As it was, perseverance to the death was perhaps, in More's view, a way of compensating for his absence from the churchly hierarchy in its time of gravest need. But these are tenuous conjectures: all we know is that he performed a service unusual for a layman by writing treatises against heresy.

❖

Fury against heresy there certainly was in his writings, but our assessment of this quality needs to be tempered by the humane, humanist, Socratic portrait drawn by Chambers and by the devotional, humanist, juridical, and statesmanlike portraits drawn by Holbein. But how can this be done? How can one defend or explain the violence of More's manner in his works of religious controversy? Professor Elton has put the problem well: "As William Ross, defending Henry VIII against Luther, he matched Dr. Martin in violence of abuse, a remarkable achievement. His controversial manners were bad: in his exchanges with Tyndale, he generally proved the more scurrilous of the two, and he was savage to St. German who had not been savage at all."[17] It is good to remember that More thus began his career in religious controversy by combating Luther on behalf of Henry, whose *Assertio* had been attacked by Luther in a treatise of which it has been said: "It is unlikely that any tract addressed to any king in Christian Europe had ever been as insulting, as vitriolic, as obscene as Luther's little book."[18] One might even say that More picked up his bad manners in controversy by consorting thus with Luther. More's job, willingly undertaken, to be sure, was to bespatter Luther with the same muck that Luther had hurled at Henry—only more of it, if possible. The justification for such excesses on both sides has been well stated by a later expert in religious controversy who expressly takes Luther as his model, arguing from the example of the prophets and Christ himself that there may be "a sanctified bitterness against the enemies of truth."[19]

> We all know that in private and personal injuries, yea in public sufferings for the cause of Christ, his rule and example teaches us to be so far from a readiness to speak evil, as not to answer the reviler in his language though never so much provoked. Yet in the detecting and convincing of any notorious enemy to truth and his country's peace [what More called "seditious heresy"], especially that is conceited to have a voluble and smart fluence of tongue . . . I suppose and more than suppose, it will be nothing disagreeing from Christian meekness to handle such a one in a rougher accent, and to send home his haughtiness well bespurted with his own holy-water. . . . And although in the serious uncasing of a grand imposture . . . there be mixed here and there such a grim laughter, as may appear at the same time in an austere visage, it cannot be taxed of levity or insolence: for even this vein of laughing . . . hath oft-times a strong and sinewy force in teaching and confuting; nor can there be a more proper object of indignation and scorn together than a false Prophet taken in the greatest, dearest and most dangerous cheat, the cheat of souls.[20]

That, of course, is John Milton defending his own vituperative style. The example of Milton shows that what we are watching here is a tradition of "sanctified bitterness" that runs from Luther and More on through Milton and Salmasius. This is, alas, the common practice of gifted religious humanists in verbal conflict. More and Milton and other devout humanists are using their command of good Latin and colloquial English as weapons against what they regard as deadly enemies of truth, and nothing can be too vile to sling against such vileness: the whip of cords, ingeniously and cruelly knotted, must be used to drive these evildoers out of the temple. We should not think of the typical Renaissance humanist as a peaceful person. He is an expert in language, not in self-control.

To say, however, that such vituperative violence in writing represents the real Thomas More, the inner man, seems to me as wrong as if we were to say that Milton's prose propaganda represents the real Milton, the inner man, rather than *Paradise Lost*.[21] For More is writing propaganda in the basic sense of that word, *de propaganda fide*—that is, writing to advance a certain faith or cause—and in that aim, it is not up to the writer to point out that there is much to be said for the other side. It seems to me naive to complain that More, in these writings, is unfair to the opposition, that such procedure, though appropriate to a lawyer arguing a case, is disappointing in a saint.[22] What then shall we say of St. Augustine in his polemics against the Pelagians or the Manichaeans? Even an Augustine, in polemical writing, must constrict his whole nature: the writer of polemic is of necessity ungenerous and unfair. The writing of propaganda delimits the expression of the whole being, suppresses in More the "voice of his ironic, complex sense of self," as Stephen Greenblatt has well described it; that is why More cannot display in his controversial writings his awareness of the paradoxes and ambiguities of life, and thus appears increasingly unhappy, bitter, and weary in his role as a polemicist.[23] For More the task of controversial writing, I believe, came into conflict with the sensitive inner self that Holbein found, unguarded, in one of the Windsor drawings.

We note, for example, in the *Apology*, how he seems to realize that his polemical rhetoric has carried him too far in something that, as he remembers, he has said about John Frith. He says that someone told him that "Frith labored so sore that he sweat again, in studying and writing against the blessed sacrament." More then picks up the image of the sweat and creates a bitter contrast between Frith's sweat and the bloody sweat of Christ in the Garden of Gethsemane: "I would some good friend of his should show him, that I fear me sore that Christ will kindle a fire of faggots for him, and make him therein sweat the blood out of his body here, and straight from hence send his soul for ever into the fire of hell."

More seems to realize the words are rhetorically too strong, for he then goes on to say:

> Now in these words I neither meant nor mean, that I would it were so. For so help me God and none otherwise, but as I would be glad to take more labor, loss, and bodily pain also, than peradventure many a man would wene [i.e., think], to win that young man to Christ and his true faith again, and thereby to preserve and keep him from the loss and peril of soul and body both. [*CW*, 9 : 122]

Or again, in the forty-ninth chapter of the *Apology*, in the midst of his final attack on St. German's treatise, More declares:

> As touching heretics, I hate that vice of theirs and not their persons, and very fain would I that the tone were destroyed, and the tother saved. And that I have toward no man any other mind than this (how loudly so ever these blessed new brethren, the professors and preachers of verity, belie me), if all the favor and pity that I have used

among them to their amendment were known, it would, I warrant you, well and plain appear, whereof if it were requisite I could bring forth witnesses mo than men would wene. [*CW*, 9 : 167]

Still, it is argued that—aside from Martin Luther, his only peer in vituperation—More shows intemperance in language to an unusual degree. In a sense this is true. More is wittier, more clever, more gifted in his sardonic command of language than most writers of controversy. His vituperation stands out because of this literary power, not because of any unusual vindictiveness in his person. His opponents would have shown equal vituperative power if they had had the ability to do so. And Luther did. But Tyndale surely, one might argue, was a verbal artist of the very greatest power, as his translation of the Bible proves: he had consummate skill in rendering profound thought in common language. But in vituperation Tyndale has no gift. When he tries, he sounds only petulant; his strength lies elsewhere. We can see this in the exchanges between More and Tyndale set forth in More's *Confutation of Tyndale's Answer*.

When Tyndale tries to be vituperative, More can perform cadenzas around him, as when Tyndale scornfully refers to Erasmus as More's "darling" and More launches into a brilliant cascade of rhetorical buffoonery on the theme of "Erasmus my darling" (*CW*, 8 : 177)—or when Tyndale unwisely brings in the "filthy idol Priapus" to ridicule the sacrament of confession, thus giving More another chance to take off on the theme of Luther, his nun, and the "abominable bitchery" of the newly married priests (*CW*, 8 : 207).[24] On the other hand, when Tyndale is setting forth reformed doctrine in his style of sturdy, simple eloquence, More's answers frequently are labored and he comes out second best.[25]

As for More's savagery against the mild St. German, we may

well wonder about the mildness of this "pacifier," as More calls him, and we may understand More's sarcasm in the *Apology* when he takes this mild, pacific pose to be a mask that guards a ruthless attack upon the privileges of the Church. More seems to suspect that the anonymous treatise "concerning the division between the spirituality and temporality"—almost certainly the work of Christopher St. German, as More almost certainly realized—was part of an official campaign designed by Thomas Cromwell to undermine the Church and in the end take over most of its powers and properties.[26] Against this threat More adopts the device of writing his own *Apology*: his defense of his own writings and actions against the heretics. Tacitly More is saying, "This treatise on the 'division' represents everything that I have tried to combat." Suspecting, though, that this publication is coming from a source quite close to the throne, More, in his usual devious way, does not compose his *Apology* as a direct attack on St. German's *Division*. No, he brings in this attack only by the way, as part of a long list of charges that have been brought against him by "the brethren," who "find first for a great fault, that my writing is over-long, and therefore too tedious to read. For which cause they say they will never once vouchsafe to look thereon" (*CW*, 9:5). This charge seems to have hit a sore spot in More, for he keeps returning to it, and indeed, who can deny that the *Confutation* is over-long? In spite of their declaration that they will never look upon the book, the brethren seem to have found lots of particular flaws within the text.

> They find a great fault, that I handle Tyndale and Barnes, their two new gospellers, with no fairer words nor in no more courteous manner.
>
> And over this I write, they say, in such wise, that I show myself suspect in the matter and partial toward the clergy.

And then they say that my works were worthy much more credence, if I had written more indifferently, and had declared and made open to the people the faults of the clergy.

Now, at last, after these preliminaries, he comes to St. German's treatise: "And in this point they lay for a sample the goodly and godly mild and gentle fashion used by him, whosoever he was, that now lately wrote the book of the division between the temporality and the spirituality, which charitable mild manner they say that if I had used, my works would have been read both of many mo and with much better will" (*CW*, 9:5). He then adds a few other charges. But More delays dealing with St. German's treatise until eight and a half chapters have elapsed—forty pages, a quarter of the *Apology*. And although he spends most of the remaining three-quarters of the *Apology* attacking this treatise, he says that he is not going to do so. On page sixty-one,[27] for example, he says: "But forasmuch as the touching of the book is here not my principal purpose, I will therefore not peruse it over and touch every point thereof. Which if I would, I could, I think, well make men see that very few parts thereof had either such charity or such indifferency therein, as not only the new naughty bretherhed boasteth, but some good folk also take it at a superficial reading." He then, of course, proceeds to prove exactly this. It turns out that he has, well, one more thing, and yet one more thing, to add against St. German's treatise until, one hundred and twenty pages later, he comes to the forty-ninth chapter, which opens with words that have the effect of a double take: "And thus, good Christian readers, I make an end of this matter, the book, I mean, of this division" (*CW*, 9:167). And then after four more pages of making an end, wholly concerned with denouncing the book, he adds a final two-page chapter coming back to "the last fault that the brethren find in my books."

More's *Apology* is thus composed according to a series of maneuvers designed to distract readers from thinking that this treatise on the division is something he is deliberately attacking; no, his attack happens only by the way, in defense of himself and as an example of how misguided and perhaps well-intentioned people may help to spread trouble even though they mean to spread peace:

> For truth it is that murmur and dissension (God knoweth how it began) against the clergy is a great way gone onward in his unhappy journey, and may by such manner and mean of pacifying, within short process be conveyed round about the realm, and leave no place in peace. Not that I would think the man that made that book to be of such malicious mind, as willingly to sow dissension, but that, as me seemeth, he taketh at the leastwise unware a wrong way toward the contrary, and that the manner of his handling is far from such indifferency as he should use, that would make a love day and appease any murmur and grudge of the lay people against the priests. [*CW*, 9:54–55]

The *Apology*, with its pervasive irony and indirection, is one of More's most skillful pieces of improvised ordering under the guise of a casual disorder. Its mode of indirection takes us back to that famous passage in More's *Utopia*, where the character named Morus is trying to persuade Hythlodaeus that philosophers should take part in the councils of kings. In answer to Hythlodaeus's stern objection, this character called More argues:

> By the indirect approach you must seek and strive to the best of your power to handle matters tactfully. What you cannot turn to good you must make as little bad as you can. For it is impossible that all should be well unless all men

were good, a situation which I do not expect for a great
many years to come!

But Hythlodaeus then gives the grim prophetic answer a dozen
years before More's troubles began:

> As to that indirect approach of yours, I cannot see its rele-
> vancy. . . . At court there is no room for dissembling, nor
> may one shut one's eyes to things. One must openly ap-
> prove the worst counsels and subscribe to the most ruinous
> decrees. He would be counted a spy and almost a traitor,
> who gives only faint praise to evil counsels.[28]

In the end More's indirect approach could not conceal from
Cromwell and the King his bitter and continuing opposition to
what they were attempting to achieve. He went to his death because the King, angered by More's refusal to submit, saw him
as a spy, a traitor, and an ungrateful servant. But, as More said
in his last words on the scaffold, the inner man maintained a
higher loyalty.

2

The Order of the Heart

M ore's *Confutation of Tyndale's Answer* is the most neglected of all his major works. Complaints against its great length and tediousness are of long standing, arising from the earliest readers (or non-readers), as More testifies in the opening chapters of his *Apology*. But then, More says, "Every way seemeth long to him that is weary ere he begin."[1]

I would like to provide some reasons to prevent such weariness from arising when readers face the three thick volumes in the new edition of the *Confutation*.[2] For More goes on to explain that the great length stems in part from his awareness that many of his readers "would peradventure wax weary to read over a long book, and therefore have I taken the more pain upon every chapter, to the intent that they shall not need to read over any chapter but one, and that it shall not force greatly which one throughout all the book" (*CW*, 8 : 9–10). More is explaining that of course he never expected all his readers to read all of his book. It is addressed to the unlearned who, he feels, have been seduced by certain arguments of Tyndale and his sect, arguments that they have heard in sermons or in private discussions, or which they have read in the many short treatises circulated by the brethren. More's aim is to take each argument separately, show its fallacy, and at the same time make it representative of the erroneous drift of the whole movement:

> Now he that will therefore read any one chapter, either at adventure, or else some chosen piece in which himself had went [i.e., thought] that his evangelical father Tyndale had said wonderful well, or else friar Barnes either, when he shall in that one chapter, as I am sure he shall, find his holy prophet plainly proved a fool, he may be soon eased of any farther labor. For then hath he good cause to cast him quite off and never meddle more with him; and then shall he

never need to read more of my book neither, and so shall he make it short enough. [*CW*, 8 : 10]

Such a reading of any one chapter is made all the more effective by the method of argument that More has described a page or so earlier:

And I sometime take the pain to rehearse some one thing in divers fashions in mo places than one, because I would that the reader should, in every place where he fortuneth to fall in reading, have at his hand, without remitting over elsewhere or labor of farther seeking for it, as much as shall seem requisite for that matter that he there hath in hand. And therein the labor of all that length is mine own, for ease and shortening of the reader's pain. [*CW*, 8 : 8]

In other words, More has composed here a compendium of essays in confutation, giving each essay a certain completeness of its own. Thus any person, parson, head of a family, or friend who is worried about the tendencies in himself or in others to accept the arguments of these new men may use each chapter to confute any given point that may arise at any time in any group or in any solitary meditation. Meanwhile the essays are linked together by the repetition of identical arguments and identical phrases, clauses, and sentences, running like a litany throughout the work. This understanding of the *Apology's* overall structure will help to explain the continual repetition of certain set themes, as, for example, the theme that Tyndale's heresy encourages and defends the marriage of a monk and a nun—More's constant jibe, often given in the most virulent language:

For he [God] hath suffered them of his high goodness to show themself at last, and to fall into such open beastly faults, friars and nuns creeping to bed together, and then to preach and teach their shameless lechery boldly about for

good and lawful matrimony, that they have thereby now
set out their gear so sightly that every man may well and
plainly see such open ribaldry with his own eyes, and well
and easily judge the thing for sin and beastly bitchery, and
the defence thereof for a shameful shameless heresy, and
the preachers thereof for more than monstrous heretics.
[*CW*, 8 : 140]

This theme should not be taken as evidence of some pu-
ritanical obsession in More. It is part of his general pattern of
repetition, but it becomes prominent because it provides such an
open field for the play of More's mordant, earthy wit, and also
because it provides a riposte against the reformers' charges of
moral laxity in the Roman church. More adopts the strategy of
pointing out that this breaking of vows in the Lutheran sect is
not an occasional or intermittent lapse, but is in fact an openly
avowed principle: that it is *right* for a monk to wed a nun, that
it is *right* to break monastic vows. Now which would you prefer, he asks by implication, would you prefer these admitted,
occasional, undefended, and frequently denounced lapses among
the present clergy, or would you prefer the practice of this new
sect that raises these lapses, this breaking of vows, to the level of
a basic principle of life?

For this open heresy of friars' filthy matrimony giveth us
so plain and open warning of their worldly fleshly devilish
spirit, so plain against all holy scripture and all good honest
men: that we never could have excuse afore God if we
would give such preachers, so bold in such ribaldry, either
faith or credence or favorable hearing: namely sith there
was never in all Christendom, sith the faith first began, any
holy doctor, nor doctor good or bad, before Luther's days,
that any thing hath written, but he hath abhorred and de-
tested it to the devil of hell, that ever any person, either

> man or woman, that hath vowed themself monk, friar, or
> nun, should afterward run out of their religion, cast their
> vow at their back, and fall to flesh and wed. [*CW*,
> 8 : 140–41]

More of course is not attacking matrimony; he is attacking what he calls "contempt of their holy vows made before to God. . . . All good honest people of Christendom this fifteen hundreth year have had such beastly wedding in great abomination" (*CW*, 8 : 141). Here is another of More's repeated themes and phrases: these new men are flying in the face of the practice and belief "of Christendom this fifteen hundreth year."

Such repetitions, then, have a threefold function. They in-sure that the reader who reads only one section will find there all the main points of More's *Confutation*; they reinforce, blow after blow, each single point for those who read at greater length; and they gradually bind all the essays in confutation into a unity.

It will be a unity of the kind that one finds in Augustine's *De Trinitate* or in his *Ten Sermons on the First Epistle of St. John*. For these are not so much treatises as they are groups of essays or homilies on a set theme, growing toward a unity of meaning by repetition, recapitulation, association, even by digression. One thinks of the great *Pensée* of Pascal (no. 283), in which Jacques Maritain has seen the essential difference between the writings of Augustine and Aquinas:

> The heart has its own order; the intellect has its own, which
> is by principle and demonstration. The heart has another.
> We do not prove that we ought to be loved by enumerating
> in order the causes of love; that would be ridiculous. Jesus
> Christ and Saint Paul employ the rule of love, not of intel-
> lect; for they would warm, not instruct. It is the same with
> Saint Augustine. This order consists chiefly in digressions

on each point to indicate the end, and keep it always in sight.[3]

"Cet ordre consiste principalement à la digression sur chaque point qu'on rapporte à la fin, pour la montrer toujours." One thinks of More's digression on the proper use of *no* and *nay*, where he apologizes at the outset for considering such a "trifle" and says he would "not here note by the way" such an error, except that it shows how a man who can make such a mistake in the use of "two so plain English words" is hardly a suitable person to translate the Bible into English. More, always the purist, then explains, in accordance with the grammar of his day, the proper use of these two words in answering a question:

"Nay" answereth the question framed by the affirmative. As for ensample, if a man should ask Tyndale himself: is an heretic meet to translate holy scripture into English? Lo, to this question if he will answer true English, he must answer "nay" and not "no". But and if the question be asked him thus, lo: is not an heretic meet to translate holy scripture into English? To this question, lo, if he will answer true English, he must answer "no" and not "nay". And a like difference is there between these two adverbs, "ye", and "yes". For if the question be framed unto Tyndale by the affirmative in this fashion: if an heretic falsely translate the New Testament into English, to make his false heresies seem the word of God, be his books worthy to be burned? To this question asked in this wise, if he will answer true English he must answer "ye" and not "yes". But now if the question be asked him thus, lo, by the negative: if an heretic falsely translate the New Testament into English, to make his false heresies seem the word of God, be not his books well worthy to be burned? To this question in this fashion framed if he will answer true English, he may not answer "ye", but he must answer "yes", and say, "Yes, mary, be they, both the translation and the translator, and all that will hold with them."

And this thing, lo, though it be no great matter, yet I have thought good to give Tyndale warning of, because I would have him write true one way or other, that though I cannot make him by no mean to write true matter, I would have him yet at the leastwise write true English.

But now to the matter self. [*CW*, 8 : 731–32]

I think we can agree that More has here not forgotten the ultimate end of his confutation. Similarly he keeps his eye on the end in what is perhaps the most extravagant example of his repetitive technique, his digression on "Erasmus my darling":

Then he asketh me why I have not contended with Erasmus, whom he calleth my darling of all this long while, for translating of this word *ecclesia* into this word *congregatio.* And then he cometh forth with his feat proper taunt, that I favor him of likelihed for making of his book of *Moria* in my house. There had he hit me, lo, save for lack of a little salt. I have not contended with Erasmus my darling because I found no such malicious intent with Erasmus my darling as I find with Tyndale. For had I found with Erasmus my darling the shrewd intent and purpose that I find in Tyndale: Erasmus my darling should be no more my darling. But I find in Erasmus my darling that he detesteth and abhorreth the errors and heresies that Tyndale plainly teacheth and abideth by, and therefore Erasmus my darling shall be my dear darling still. And surely if Tyndale had either never taught them, or yet had the grace to revoke them: then should Tyndale be my dear darling too. But while he holdeth such heresies still, I cannot take for my darling him that the devil taketh for his darling. [*CW*, 8 : 177]

From the very beginning of this series of adroit repetitions, More has never lost sight of the end: that Tyndale is the devil's darling.

Throughout the *Confutation* one can see and hear this Augustinian way of working, a way that More must have learned from a saturation in Augustine's writings very early in his life. We remember that at the age of twenty-three he was lecturing in London on Augustine's *City of God*, with Grocyn in the audience. This analogy in method with Augustine's writings is reinforced by the way in which Augustine is called up as a witness in the *Confutation* twenty times more often and at much greater length than any other father of the church. This is especially evident in the conclusion to More's first volume—that is, the ending of the third book of the *Confutation*, where More defends the unwritten traditions of the church by calling upon ten of the "old holy doctors" (another of his constant refrains); chief among them is Augustine, whose words occupy three of the six pages devoted to these testimonies, including a long translation from the *Confessions*.

This method, both in Augustine and in More, derives from a deep-seated conviction (or perhaps we should call it an instinct) about the ways in which truth may be found. It is a principle based upon Augustine's view of the workings of the will, which in his psychology takes priority over the intellect. Conversely, Tyndale believes that the intellect is predominant and that once the intellect has seen the truth, the will always follows. This difference in principle creates a difference in the styles of More and Tyndale. For More, following Augustine, believes that truth will not be found through the relentless logic of Tyndale, which, proceeding from the doctrine of justification by faith, rides with brilliant wit and vehement persuasive power over all obstacles that deny or defy that premise. More's repetitive, digressive essays interrupt the onward striding of this logic, breaking its step, knocking it off stride, by bringing forward in an Augustinian manner an Augustinian view of life and religion—a view that sees, not a church of "elects" who cannot fall to damnation, however they may slip, but a church of fallen people, any one of whom has yet available the hope of redemption. This is the heart of More's objection to Tyndale: that his doctrine diminishes hope and changes that gracious word *charity* to a dubious, highly fallible word *love*—a word that, as More sees it, can as well turn to lechery as to the love of God.

Can we not, perhaps, without at all equating the views of Aquinas and Tyndale, see something of Pascal's distinction between the order of the heart and the order of the intellect as we read the *Confutation of Tyndale's Answer?* More's practice of quoting Tyndale at length, and accurately, is, as he says in chapter 2 of the *Apology,* an effort to avoid the method of tendentious summary that Tyndale has used in answering More. More himself is determined to set forth his opponent's views exactly, and so he increases the length of his work by long and exact quotations from Tyndale. The effect of this method is dramatic, for it sets up a constant dialogue between Tyndale and More—a dialogue in which the voice of More's opponent emerges in all its immense persuasive power.

More is well aware that Tyndale is a formidable opponent in this literary combat, for he warns at the outset against Tyndale's "heap of high vehement words": "Let not therefore Tyndale (good reader) with his gay glorious words carry you so fast and so far away, but that ye remember to pull him back by the sleeve a little" (*CW,* 8 : 48). What More must show is that, however plausible, persuasive, and convincing the voice of this literary artist may be, his words are lies because his doctrine is false. Yet dialogue is perhaps not quite the right word for this contest, since the two voices are not exactly speaking to each other: each speaker, while acutely aware of his opponent's presence, is speaking directly to us, using every device known to the art of homily and oratory. Let us see how it works in one self-contained section, the part dealing with satisfaction for sins—a section that occurs within a thirty-five-page discussion of the sacraments that More calls a "long digression"! (*CW*, 8:120).

More well knows that here is the heart of Tyndale's attack on the ancient practices of the church, and so he introduces the problem with a brief prologue that makes clear the direction of Tyndale's theme:

> He will that we shall for our sins no more but only re-pent. For as for going about to punish ourself any thing for our own sins, by penance doing, with fasting, prayer, alms deed, or any bodily affliction, that God may have the more mercy upon us, which thing all good Christian people have ever used to do, and which the church calleth satisfaction: this thing Tyndale calleth as ye shall hear. [*CW*, 8:89–90]

Then the debate begins, with the names Tyndale and More set off in the middle of the page, to mark the dramatic speaker. Tyndale opens thus: "Sin we through fagility never so oft, yet as soon as we repent and come into the right way again, and unto the testament which God hath made in Christ's blood: our sins vanish away as smoke in the wind, and as darkness at the coming of light, or as thou cast a little blood or milk into the main sea" (*CW*, 8:90). Note the eloquence of that series of lengthening, parallel similes: "our sins vanish away as smoke in the wind, and as darkness at the coming of light, or as thou cast a little blood or milk into the main sea." Thus the power of Christ's blood is fully established. Now what is the logical consequence of such power? It is this, says Tyndale in the next sentence: "Insomuch that whoever goeth about to make satisfaction for his sins to godward, saying in his heart, thus much have I sinned, thus much will I do again [i.e., in return], or this wise will I live to make amends withal, or this will I do to get heaven withal: the same is an infidel, faithless, and damned in his deed-doing, and hath lost his part in Christ's blood, because he is disobedient unto God's testament, and setteth up another of his own imagination, unto which he will compel God to obey." Such a one is "damned in his deed-doing" because the doing of such deeds has no merit toward salvation. But what then about good deeds, we may ask, should we not do them? The answer follows logically in Tyndale's next sentence: "If we love God: we have a commandment to love our neighbor also, as saith John in his pistle. And if we have offended him [i.e., our neighbor] to make him amends, or if we have not where-with, to ask him forgiveness, and to do and to suffer all things for his sake to win him to God and to nourish peace and unity: but to godward Christ is an everlasting satisfaction and ever sufficient." Notice the resonant eloquence of the balanced phrasing and sound effects of that conclusion: "everlasting satisfaction and ever sufficient" (*CW*, 8 : 90).

Formidable logic, vehement words, glorious words. "The beginning of these words seem very godly," says More, "for the magnifying of the great mercy of God." But consider closely the consequences of such an easy doctrine of forgiveness: "Neither purgatory need to be feared when we go hence, nor penance need to be done while we be here, but sin and be sorry and sit and make merry, and then sin again and then repent a little and run to the ale and wash away the sin, think once on God's promise and then do what we list [i.e., like]. For hoping sure in that, kill we ten men on a day, we cast but a little blood into the main sea" (*CW*, 8 : 90–91). So More begins to demolish the effect of the grand rhetorical comparisons in Tyndale's first sentence. More then goes on to analyse the falsity of the doctrinal charge implied here, saying that Tyndale "is not so foolish but that he knoweth well enough that all Christian men believe that

no penance is of itself sufficient for the least sin, but the passion
and pain of Christ maketh our penance available [i.e., effectual]."
Thus More's doctrinal position is established in the exact middle
of his reply. Then More turns sharply to consider this new doctrine of salvation by "no more but faith." And he asks Tyndale
what he means by the word "repenting": "a little short sorrow,
or a great sorrow and a long?" If he means "a great fervent sorrow with grief and trouble of mind," then, says More, this
heresy is nothing much to be worried about:

> For no doubt is it but that Tyndale's tale to such a man
> shall seem, God wot, full fond [i.e., foolish]. For he that
> hath such repentance will to shrift, I warrant you, and take
> penance of the priest, and do much more thereto, what-
> soever Tyndale tell him. And he that is christened and
> careth for no shrift repenteth never a deal, but they that
> repent not at all be Tyndale's repentant sinners. [*CW*,
> 8:91]

Now More is ready for his finale. He concludes with a crushing
piece of bitter and indecent wit that plays once again upon the
eloquent ending of Tyndale's first sentence:

> Will ye see that it is so? Go me to Martin Luther, the
> first master of Tyndale in this matter, though now his
> scholar passeth him. While that friar lieth with his nun, and
> woteth well he doth naught [i.e., evil], and saith still he
> doth well: let Tyndale tell me what repenting is that. He
> repenteth every morning, and to bed again every night,
> thinketh on God's promise first, and then go sin again upon
> trust of God's testament; and then he calleth it casting of a
> little milk into the main sea. [*CW*, 8:91–92]

With that closing innuendo More uses his characteristic repetition of theme to destroy the power of Tyndale's rhetoric. His

manner of proceeding by repetition and digression may be found throughout his literary career, whether in short passages or in long works. Thus the *Dialogue of Comfort* opens with the powerful threat of persecution, but the imminence of that threat gradually recedes throughout the short opening book. In the second book, twice as long as the first, the theme of persecution disappears, as More goes on to deal with every other conceivable form of tribulation. Then at the outset of Book III the threat of persecution returns with redoubled force and joins with the repeated text of Psalm 90 to knit the whole work together in an Augustinian way.

So, too, the English treatise on the Passion begins as though it were going to be just another of the many meditations on the life of Christ that have come down from the Middle Ages, following the ancient threefold method: quotation of Scripture, exposition, and prayer. But gradually it appears that this is another kind of "answer" to the "poisoned book": a sequel to More's last work of controversy, *The answer to the first part of the poisoned book, which a nameless heretic hath named the supper of the Lord* (December 1533). Here More has confuted the denial of the real presence of Christ in the Eucharist, using two modes of writing; first, in a long opening chapter (a third of the treatise) he has engaged in his first extended piece of biblical exegesis, as he refutes the interpretation of the sixth chapter of John's gospel given by the "nameless heretic" whom he sardonically calls "Master Masker." After this relatively temperate and judicious exposition More devotes the last two-thirds of the work to the sort of line-by-line dissection that he has used in confuting Tyndale, with similarly vitriolic language. As the editors of the new edition of the *Answer* observe, "After the riches of positive biblical exposition in Book I, the return to the hurly-burly of the polemical style in the final four books seems like a fall from grace."[4]

In the preface to the *Answer* More promises a "second part" of this confutation, dealing with the institution of the Last Supper as a sacrament (*CW*, 11 : 10). It looks as though the English treatise on the Passion is this second part.[5] But if so, why does More lay aside the polemical mode that he has used in his earlier answer? More has clearly decided to pursue a different approach to dealing with heresy: the translation of Scripture and interpretation based directly upon Scripture, as he has done in the first chapter of the *Answer*. Thus, in his own way, More is doing what Tyndale challenged the church in England to do: make the Bible available to all in their own tongue. As Louis Schuster has said (*CW*, 8 : 1165), we can now see that the only effective response to Tyndale's translation of the Bible, with its controversial glosses, lay in an authorized translation with authorized glosses.

Has More begun to realize that his controversial weapons, however skillfully wielded, are not having their desired effect? One senses in the *Apology*, as in the *Answer to the First Part of the Poisoned Book*, a weariness, a sad realization that the flood of heretical books is sweeping on, despite his careful, lengthy confutations. In the end More, like Tyndale, turns to the Word and lets it speak in the form of his terse and simple translations from Gerson's harmony of the four Gospels, the *Monotessaron*.

More's commentary in his English treatise on the Passion takes the form of a series of well-rounded essays, or "lectures," as More calls them—"lectures" in the old sense of exploratory readings into the meaning of a given text. These lectures grow together on the theme developed near the close of the very first lecture, in words that recall the central theme of his *Answer to the First Part of the Poisoned Book*. More says that Christ "will that we shall receive the holy Paschal Lamb, his own blessed body, both bodily in the blessed sacrament, and spiritually with faith, hope, and charity receive it worthily, and in such wise also virtually, when we receive it not sacramentally."[6] That is, we receive it effectually—"virtually"—when we are in devout attendance at the Mass. Then, giving an allegorical interpretation to the details of the Old Testament ritual, More gives directions for the proper reception of the sacrament. All this prepares the way for the final lecture in this English treatise, which tells "in what manner wise we ought to use ourself in the receiving" and then ends, as I have argued elsewhere,[7] with the little treatise that William Rastell printed separately, the treatise "To receive the blessed body of our Lord, sacramentally and virtually both."

I do not mean to argue that More planned at the outset to end his essays on the Passion at this point. Rastell prints a long title which shows that More planned to extend his commentary on through the burial in the sepulcher. But in the actual course of his writing More came, it seems, by the Augustinian way of exploration, to discover his ending sooner than he had anticipated. He therefore seems to have discarded the long title and the proposed preface, of which Rastell prints a fragment (*CW*, 13 : 3). These materials do not exist in any known manuscript, though Rastell undoubtedly found them among More's papers. If we read the English treatise on the Passion as the work appears in both manuscripts, without these materials at the head but always followed by the short treatise on receiving the sacrament, then the work has a beautiful completeness. It is an *Answer to the Poisoned Book* more temperate, more carefully devised, more effectually conceived and performed than the answer to the first part. This English treatise on the Passion was, we now know, a work written in large part, and perhaps entirely, before More entered the Tower of London (*CW*, 13 : xxxix–xli); and with this work his public duty as author is completed.

What remains he wrote primarily for himself, for his family, and for the diminishing few who may share his views. One need not doubt that More hoped that a larger audience might sometime come to read what seem to be his last two major works: the *Dialogue of Comfort* and the *De Tristitia*. Yet both these works, under the guise of a public voice, speak primarily to the inner man. In both the basic theme is the problem of enduring persecution to the death. It is the subject that begins and ends the *Dialogue of Comfort*, despite its long excursus into other matters during the middle book. Perhaps this middle book, with all its merry tales and varied anecdotes, is an attempt to cloak the deeper, inner theme.

In the *De Tristitia* the problem of the cautious, fearful martyr is introduced very early in the work, on the eleventh leaf of the Valencia manuscript, near the beginning of More's meditation on the text, "Tristis est anima mea usque ad mortem."

> He suddenly felt such a sharp and bitter attack of sadness, grief, fear, and weariness that He immediately uttered, even in their presence, those anguished words which gave expression to His overburdened feelings: "My soul is sad unto death." . . . He knew that His ordeal was now imminent and just about to overtake Him: the treacherous betrayer, the bitter enemies, binding ropes, false accusations, slanders, blows, thorns, nails, the cross, and horrible tortures stretched out over many hours.[8]

All this mental suffering of Christ in the Garden, More says, was endured in order to provide the fearful with an example: "Therefore, since He foresaw that there would be many people of such a delicate constitution that they would be convulsed with terror at any danger of being tortured, He chose to enhearten them by the example of His own sorrow, His own sadness, His own weariness and unequalled fear" (*CW*, 14:101). And so, for seventeen leaves in the Valencia manuscript, leaves heavily revised, deeply reconsidered, More ponders this problem of the fearful martyr until, at the close of this section, the meditating mind hears the inward speaking of Christ to the fearful soul, saying, "O faint of heart, take courage and do not despair" (*CW*, 14 : 101–03).

But then, as More prepares to take up the next biblical passage, he moves abruptly away from any such problem; he turns from the inward self back to the outer world, saying, "Reader, let us pause for a little at this point and contemplate with a devout mind our commander lying on the ground in humble supplication" (*CW*, 14 : 113–15). For the next sixteen leaves, he proceeds to give an objective discourse on the proper attitudes of prayer, couched in very familiar address to the reader. "And then our actions too, in how many ways do they betray that our minds are wandering miles away? We scratch our heads, clean our fingernails with a pocketknife, pick our noses with our fingers, meanwhile making the wrong responses. Having no idea what we have already said and what we have not said, we make a wild guess as to what remains to be said" (*CW*, 14 : 127). Imagine yourself (he adds) standing before "some mortal prince or other who has your life in his hands," pleading for pardon for some crime:

> Now, when you have been brought into the presence of
> the prince, go ahead and speak to him carelessly, casually,
> without the least concern. While he stays in one place and
> listens attentively, stroll around here and there as you run
> through your plea. Then, when you have had enough of
> walking up and down, sit down on a chair. . . . Then yawn,
> stretch, sneeze, spit without giving it a thought, and belch
> up the fumes of your gluttony. . . .
>
> Tell me now, what success could you hope for from such
> a plea as this? [*CW*, 14 : 129–33]

How could such a witty, teasing tone come from a man worrying about his own imminent torture and death? Perhaps we have misunderstood the preceding section on the fearful martyr; perhaps this treatise, just like the *Dialogue of Comfort*, is objective, addressed to Hungarians, has little to do with the individual situation of More, whose prayers surely never were performed in such a fashion. The next section continues this objectivity while considering the theological problem of how Christ speaks both as God and as man. Here again, More uses the familiar manner of address: "But perhaps some meticulous fussy dissector of the divine plan might say . . . 'Since He was God, could He not at one and the same time speak the command and insure its execution?' Doubtless He could have, my good man," says More, "since He was God, Who carried out whatever He wished, Who created all things with a word" (*CW*, 14 : 197). But for his own reasons God did not choose to proceed in this way.

From here More shifts briefly into the mode of controversy, denouncing the "pernicious nonsense" of those "shameless men" who "contend that it is futile for anyone to seek the intercession of any angel or departed saint" (*CW*, 14 : 223–25). But shortly after this, when he begins to meditate upon Christ's bloody sweat, More returns with redoubled attention to the problems of the fearful martyr for five of the most heavily revised leaves in the entire manuscript (folios 59–63)—leaves which show again the acute attention that More is giving to this issue.

Then, in the next section, the meditation moves again toward the outer world, as More uses the sleeping of the disciples as an occasion to denounce negligent bishops who are asleep in the face of dangers to their flock, or worse: "Rather they are numbed and buried in destructive desires; that is, drunk with the new wine of the devil, the flesh, and the world, they sleep like pigs sprawling in the mire" (*CW*, 14 : 263). After this More embarks on a long, witty, Erasmian discussion of the uses of irony in Christ's words, "Why are you sleeping? Sleep on now and take your rest'' (*CW*, 18 : 287). Other objective matters follow, culminating in the long passage of controversy arising from the scene of the betrayal of Christ by the kiss of Judas:

> I think we would not be far wrong if we were to fear that the time approaches when the son of man, Christ, will be betrayed into the hands of sinners, as often as we see an imminent danger that the mystical body of Christ, the church of Christ, namely the Christian people, will be brought to ruin at the hands of wicked men. And this, alas, for some centuries now we have not failed to see happening somewhere, now in one place, now in another, while the cruel Turks invade some parts of the Christian dominion and other parts are torn asunder by the internal strife of manifold heretical sects.
>
> Whenever we see such things or hear they are beginning to happen, however far away, let us think that this is no time for us to sit and sleep but rather to get up immediately and bring relief to the danger of others in whatever way we can, by our prayers at least if in no other way. Nor is such danger to be taken lightly because it happens at some distance from us. . . . For we have reason to fear that the destructive force will make its way from them to us. . . .
> [*CW*, 14 : 345–49]

Above all, More goes on to say, "Christ is betrayed into the hands of sinners in a special way among those of a certain sect . . . [who] altogether deny that the real body of Christ [corpus Christi] is contained in the sacrament, though they call it by that name'' (*CW*, 14 : 355). This sort of contagion, More warns in conclusion,

> spreads gradually and imperceptibly while those persons who despise it at first, afterwards can stand to hear it and

respond to it with less than full scorn, then come to tolerate
wicked discussions, and afterwards are carried away into
error, until like a cancer (as the apostle says) the creeping
disease finally takes over the whole country. . . . But so
much for my digression into these mysteries; let us now
return to the historical events. [CW, 14 : 359–61]

Digression indeed: this passage gives the central motive for
Thomas More's incarceration in the Tower and the central motive for his meditation on the agony of Christ.

The treatise ends with puzzling abruptness in two brief leaves
under the final heading, "De christi captione" ("On the Capture
of Christ"). This unexpected ending might lead one to think
that the treatise is unfinished, as William Rastell thought when
he wrote after the final words: "Sir Thomas More wrote no
more of this work: for when he had written this far, he was in
prison kept so strait, that all his books and pen and ink and
paper was taken from him, and soon after was he put to death"
(CW, 14 : 1165). We have no reason to doubt that this was so.
On the other hand, the matter-of-fact nature of the contents
may be More's way of reasserting his mask of objectivity. These
final pages constitute what might be called a long footnote:

Exactly when they first laid hands on Jesus is a point on
which the experts disagree. . . . For Matthew and Mark re-
late the events in such an order as to allow the conjecture
that they laid hands on Jesus immediately after Judas' kiss.
And this is the opinion adopted not only by many celebrated doctors of the church but also approved by that remarkable man John Gerson, who follows it in presenting
the sequence of events in his work entitled *Monotessaron*
(the work which I have generally followed in enumerating
the events of the passion in this discussion). But in this one
place I have departed from him. [CW, 14 : 619–23]

More has transferred to this place the words, "Tunc ac-
cesserunt et manus iniecerunt in Iesum" ("Then they came up
and laid hands on Jesus") from a place that came much earlier in
Gerson's treatise.[9] Why? It seems possible that More was quite
deliberately creating this abrupt dramatic ending, for he moves
out of his objective scholarly tone toward a grand crescendo,
with a great sweep of the best Renaissance Latin, a conclusion in
which, while allegedly only fixing the time when the capture of
Christ occurred, he makes three indispensable points. First, he
stresses the physical power of Christ, by which he could have
prevented all this from happening. Second, he stresses the
power of Christ to save his apostles and the young man whom
More has earlier declared to be an image of the Christian soul
escaping from earth to heaven. And finally, he shows that
Christ has willingly allowed his final suffering for our good. I
will quote this concluding passage in the old translation by
More's granddaughter, Mary Basset, where we may almost
hear the voice of More speaking in the language of his day:

> Nevertheless, in this one thing varying from his opinion, I
> have deemed it better to be of their mind which are right
> notable writers too, that upon very probable reasons
> gathered of the words of St. Luke and St. John the Evange-
> list do suppose that after Judas had kissed our Lord and was
> returned back to the soldiers and the Jews again, and after
> they were all with the only words of Christ stricken down
> flat to the ground, and after the chief priest's servant's ear
> was cut off and made whole by Christ afresh, and after he
> had rebuked Peter for his fighting and stayed the rest of the
> apostles for [from?] making any resistance, and after he had
> once more spoken to the officers of the Jews that were then
> present with him and showed them that they might now at
> their pleasure take him, which erst they could never have

done, and after all the apostles were fled away, and finally after the young man whom they were not able to keep (as sure hold as they had of him) was scaped stoutly (naked as he was) from them, that then, after all this, did they first lay hands upon Jesus. [*CW*, 14 : 1165]

More's exploratory Augustinian way of working seems to have led him toward a conclusion that no amount of planning could have bettered. At this point, More might well have said, "It is finished."

3

❖ ❖ ❖ ❖ ❖ ❖ ❖ ❖ ❖

Last Letters and
A Dialogue of Comfort

More's letters from the Tower constitute our best account of his conduct during his interrogations and imprisonment, our best account of his state of mind, and some of his finest works of art—works of *art* in every sense of that word, for they show the most artful regard for the presence of several audiences. More could have no doubt that every letter he wrote might be carefully read by his keepers, perhaps even sent to Cromwell himself, who was, as More well knew, alert to any phrase which might entrap More into a confession or a recantation. One has the sense that when, for example, More is writing his account of his interrogation at Lambeth,[1] he is interested not only in sending a clear account of what happened to his daughter Margaret and thus to all his family. He is also taking the occasion to clarify and stake out his position to anyone who might happen to read the letter; meanwhile, he engages in some sharp plays of wit. "In that time saw I Master Doctor Latimer come into the garden, and there walked he with divers other doctors and chaplains of my Lord of Canterbury, and very merry I saw him, for he laughed, and took one or twain about the neck so handsomely, that if they had been women, I would have went [i.e., thought] he had been waxen wanton." Or note the apparent touch of irony in his account of how he was temporarily dumbfounded by Cranmer's argument that, in doubtful matters, one is bound to obey the king: "yet this argument seemed me suddenly so subtle and namely with such authority coming out of so noble a prelate's mouth, that I could again answer nothing thereto but only that I thought myself I might not well do so, because that in my conscience this was one of the cases in which I was bounden that I should not obey my prince." Or consider the incongruously gentle compliments that More so ceremoniously pays while recording the rough oath of Cromwell: "Upon this Master Secre-

tary (as he that tenderly favoreth me), said and sware a great
oath that he had lever [i.e., rather] that his own only son
(which is of truth a goodly young gentleman, and shall I trust
come to much worship) had lost his head than that I should thus
have refused the oath."

Later on, in a long letter which a servant secretly carried to
Dr. Wilson,[2] his fellow-prisoner in the Tower, one feels that
More's verbosity is a way of conveying the fact that he is really
unwilling to say anything to Wilson about the problem that
they both face. In one place in particular I think we can detect
more than a little mark of More's slyness, as he writes to
Wilson concerning "divers faults found in the bull of the dis-
pensation, by which the King's Council learned in the spiritual
law reckoned the bull vicious, partly for untrue suggestion,
partly by reason of unsufficient suggestion":

> Now concerning those points I never meddled. For I neither
> understand the doctors of the law nor well can turn their
> books. And many things have there since in this great
> matter grown in question wherein I neither am sufficiently
> learned in the law nor full informed of the fact and there-
> fore I am not he that either murmur or grudge, make asser-
> tions, hold opinions or keep dispicions [i.e., disputations]
> in the matter, but like the King's true, poor, humble sub-
> ject daily pray for the preservation of his Grace, and the
> Queen's Grace and their noble issue and of all the realm,
> without harm doing or intending, I thank our Lord, unto
> any man living.

More's naive ignorance of these doctors of the law may well
arouse a smile; and what shall we make of his concluding asser-
tion that he prays daily "for the preservation of his Grace, and
the Queen's Grace and their noble issue"? Which queen? Which
issue?

Most artful of all, and most important for More's *Dialogue of Comfort,* is that letter allegedly written by Margaret Roper to Alice Alington,[3] giving an account of the conversation with her father as an answer to Alice's letter relating the two fables she has been told by Audley. In a letter to Margaret in August 1534,[4] Alice (More's stepdaughter) says that Audley had come to hunt deer on her estate, and that the next day, at a neighbor's house, she took the opportunity to ask him to use his good offices to help her father. Audley was friendly enough but evaded the plea for help: "He marvelled that my father is so obstinate in his own conceit [i.e., opinion], as that everybody went forth withal save only the blind Bishop [Fisher] and he. And in good faith, said my Lord, I am very glad that I have no learning but in a few of Aesop's fables, of the which I shall tell you one." He then told her the following story:

There was a country in the which there were almost none but fools, saving a few which were wise. And they by their wisdom knew that there should fall a great rain, the which should make them all fools that should so be fouled or wet therewith. They, seeing that, made them caves under the ground till all the rain was past. Then they came forth thinking to make the fools to do what they list, and to rule them as they would. But the fools would none of that, but would have the rule themselfs for all their craft. And when the wisemen saw they could not obtain their purpose, they wished that they had been in the rain, and had defouled their clothes with them.

Audley laughed "very merrily" at the tale, but when Alice continued to plead for help for More, he told her plainly: "I would not have your father so scrupulous of his conscience. And then he told me another fable of a lion, an ass, and a wolf and of their confession."

First the lion confessed him that he had devoured all the beasts that he could come by. His confessor assoiled [i.e., absolved] him because he was a king and also it was his nature so to do. Then came the poor ass and said that he took but one straw out of his master's shoe for hunger, by the means whereof he thought that his master did take cold. His confessor could not assoil this great trespass, but by and by sent him to the bishop. Then came the wolf and made his confession, and he was straitly commanded that he should not pass sixpence at a meal. But when this said wolf had used this diet a little while, he waxed very hungry, insomuch that on a day when he saw a cow with her calf come by him, he said to himself, I am very hungry and fain would I eat, but that I am bounden by my ghostly father. Notwithstanding that, my conscience shall judge me. And then if it be so, then shall my conscience be thus, that the cow doth seem to me now but worth a groat [fourpence], and then if the cow be but worth a groat then is the calf but worth twopence. So did the wolf eat both the cow and the calf.

"I wist not what to say," Alice concludes, "for I was abashed of this answer. And I see no better suit than to Almighty God, for he is the comforter of all sorrows, and will not fail to send his comfort to his servants when they have most need."

Of the letter that Margaret sent in answer to these fables, Rastell's comment gives the right clue: "But whether this answer were written by Sir Thomas More in his daughter Roper's name, or by herself, it is not certainly known."[5] The arguments in this letter are so subtly and ironically given and the language has such a resonance of More's style that I think one ends up with very little doubt that this letter is primarily his own composition. One can imagine the father and daughter planning it together and speaking much of it aloud in More's Tower room. But its art seems to be all the father's.

This letter is a prime example of More's art of improvisation, his art of exploration, displayed at length in *A Dialogue of Comfort*. It is an art that seems informal, extemporaneous, spontaneous. It allows for long digressions, excursions, and familiar asides, but in the end it reveals, lying under and within all its apparent wandering, a firm and central line, a teleological structure based on a goal never forgotten. The chief goal of this letter is a defense of what people call More's "scruple of conscience," as described in the opening lines: "If he stand still in this scruple of his conscience (as it is at the leastwise called by many that are his friends and wise) all his friends that seem most able to do him good either shall finally forsake him, or peradventure not be able indeed to do him any good at all." "Conscience" is the key word, repeated more than forty times. The drama of the letter is set in terms of a temptation scene, with daughter Margaret in the role of "mistress Eve": "hath my daughter Alington played the serpent with you, and with a letter set you awork to come tempt your father again, and for the favor that you bear him labor to make him swear against his conscience, and so send him to the devil?"

More is thoroughly prepared to meet the temptation, for, as he says: "I have ere I came here not left unbethought nor unconsidered the very worst and the uttermost that can by possibility fall. And albeit that I know mine own frailty full well and the natural faintness of mine own heart, yet if I had not trusted that God should give me strength rather to endure all things, than offend him by swearing ungodly against mine own conscience, you may be very sure I would not have come here." After three pages carefully setting up the situation, we then find Margaret giving More her sister's letter to read: "Thereupon he read over your letter. And when he came to the end, he began it afresh and read it over again. And in the reading he made no manner haste, but advised it leisurely and pointed every word. And after that he paused, and then thus he said. . . ." Here is More in the very process of creating one of his artful improvisations. He does not speak or write spontaneously; he speaks and writes only after the line and goal of his work have been firmly established.

More now begins his answer by showing his warm appreciation of Alice's efforts to help, and especially of her "good counsel" at the end of her letter, where she expresses her faith that God "will not fail to send his comfort" in time of need. Then he shows his awareness of a possibly wider audience by declaring his confidence in the good will of both Audley and Cromwell and by pointedly urging them never to help him if he "be found other than a true man to my prince."

He next turns to Audley's first fable, which he knows all too well, he says, because Wolsey often used it in the King's Council when anyone advised against meddling in the disputes "between the Emperor and the French King." More retells the fable in Wolsey's version and concludes wryly: "But yet this fable, for his part, did in his days help the King and the realm to spend many a fair penny." As for the implications of the fable in Audley's version, More now spends over a page in showing the folly of attempting to overcome fools by becoming a fool oneself, or of hoping that a few wise men can rule a crowd of fools, or indeed of placing ultimate value upon any sort of rule except self-rule.

Then he deals with Audley's second fable, beginning with a consideration of its authorship in a tone of ironic solemnity and puzzlement that leads digressively but certainly toward a slowly dawning apprehension that he must be the scrupulous ass in Audley's view:

The second fable, Marget, seemeth not to be Aesop's. For by that the matter goeth all upon confession, it seemeth to be feigned since Christendom began. For in Greece before Christ's days they used not confession, no more the men then, than the beasts now. And Aesop was a Greek, and died long ere Christ was born. But what? Who made it maketh little matter. Nor I envy not that Aesop hath the name. But surely it is somewhat too subtle for me. For whom his Lordship understandeth by the lion and the wolf, which both twain confessed themself of ravin and devouring of all that came to their hands, and the tone enlarged his conscience at his pleasure in the construction of his penance, nor whom by the good discreet confessor that enjoined the tone a little penance, and the tother none at all, and sent the poor ass to the bishop, of all these things can I nothing tell. But by the foolish scrupulous ass, that had so sore a conscience for the taking of a straw for hunger out of his master's shoe, my Lord's other words of my scruple declare that his Lordship merrily meant that by me: signifying (as it seemeth by that similitude) that of oversight and folly, my scrupulous conscience taketh for a great perilous thing toward my soul, if I should swear this oath, which thing, as his Lordship thinketh, were indeed but a trifle.

The whole movement of this passage is characteristic of More's mode of apparently extemporaneous talking which leads the audience by irony and indirection into the very heart of the issue.

Then, after asserting his need to rely upon his own conscience, he launches into a two-page "merry" anecdote about a "poor honest man of the country that was called Company." The poor fellow would not follow the lead of "good company" but followed his own conscience instead. Margaret enlivens the tale at the outset with her show of utter ignorance concerning legal terms ("a quest of twelve men, a jury, as I remember they call it, or else a perjury"). This comic interlude, situated in the middle of the letter, proves to be the pivot on which the tone moves from comic to solemn, as Margaret continues to press her argument "that ye well ought and have good cause to change your own conscience, in conforming your own conscience to the conscience of so many other." Here is the crux of the problem, for Margaret is playing upon the old meaning of "conscience" as merely "inmost thought or conviction." But for More "conscience" is a deep moral and spiritual principle, and so in answer to her More gives a long and precise analysis of the proper relation between the law of the land and the individual conscience, a discourse that rises in eloquence until at last he reaches his ultimate declaration of faith:

> But as concerning mine own self, for thy comfort shall I say, daughter, to thee, that mine own conscience in this matter (I damn none other man's) is such as may well stand with mine own salvation. Thereof am I, Megge, so sure, as that is, God is in heaven. And therefore as for all the remnant, goods, lands, and life both (if the chance should so fortune), sith this conscience is sure for me, I verily trust in God, he shall rather strength me to bear the loss, than against this conscience to swear and put my soul in peril, sith all the causes that I perceive move other men to the contrary, seem not such unto me as in my conscience make any change.

Then he rounds out the dramatic framework by returning to the image of a temptation, saying: "How now, daughter Marget? What how, mother Eve? Where is your mind now? Sit not musing with some serpent in your breast, upon some new persuasion, to offer father Adam the apple yet once again." And so the letter concludes with the temptation firmly overcome and with Thomas More displaying, to the comfort of his friends and family, his cheerful, resolute, and loving spirit:

> And with this, my good child, I pray you heartily, be you and all your sisters, and my sons too, comfortable and serviceable to your good mother my wife. And of your good husbands' minds I have no manner doubt. Commend me to them all, and to my good daughter Alington, and to all my other friends, sisters, nieces, nephews, and allies, and unto all our servants, man, woman, and child, and all my good neighbors and our acquaintance abroad. And I right heartily pray both you and them, to serve God and be merry and rejoice in him.

This entire letter bears a very close kinship to the literary method and the contents of More's *Dialogue of Comfort.* For the letter is in itself a dialogue of comfort, an answer to Alice Alington's plea for comfort at the close of her letter, and a summation of previous conversations between More and Margaret on this very subject, as More says here near the beginning of the letter: "Daughter Margaret, we two have talked of this thing ofter than twice or thrice, and that same tale in effect that you tell me now therein, and the same fear too, have you twice told me before, and I have twice answered you too. . . ." No wonder, then, that the dialogue between father and daughter has much the same tone and manner as the longer dialogue between the two fictional Hungarians, uncle and nephew. The general subject of his dialogue-letter and *A Dialogue of Comfort* is the same: how should the Christian behave when persecutors test his strength to endure for what he believes, in his conscience, to be the true faith?

A particular analogy between the two dialogues is found in "Mother Maud's" elaborate fable of the fox, wolf, and ass, and their scruples of conscience, as told at length in the second book of *A Dialogue of Comfort*.[6] This seems to be the direct result of More's reading the similar fable in Alice Alington's letter; and More's witty and cautious reworking of the fable (omitting the Lion-King: too dangerous a topic) may be taken to represent a further and even more carefully considered answer to Audley and all others who accuse him of excessive "scrupulosity." This particular collocation lends very strong support to Rastell's statement that *A Dialogue of Comfort* was a Tower Work, as indeed its whole tenor would lead us to believe. But the parallels between this long letter and *A Dialogue of Comfort* form only one strand of the many affiliations that tie together the Tower Works into the one central work that is the ultimate achievement of all these varied writings: the preparation of More's mind to meet his death, if God so wishes.

❖

We must discount Nicholas Harpsfield's statement that *A Dialogue of Comfort* was "for the most part written with none other pen in the world than with a coal,"[7] since the Valencia manuscript of the *De Tristitia* shows that More had ample use of pen and ink in the Tower. There is no reason, then, to assume poor conditions of composition for the *Dialogue*, but rather, for More, an unusual opportunity for careful planning and writing made available by his fifteen months of lonely imprisonment. Furthermore, if we consider that the *Dialogue* bears every mark of being an ultimate spiritual testament, we may well believe that More would have lavished upon it all the care that his time would allow. The *Dialogue* itself bears out this conjecture, for it displays all the signs of More's finest literary skill, both in the details of its language and in the total command of its development. But we must, to appreciate its skill, adjust ourselves to its unhurried, deliberate pace and to its highly colloquial style, which the Corpus Christi manuscript accentuates.

The dialogue is set in Hungary, where two Hungarians, Uncle Antony and his nephew Vincent, discuss the problems of human suffering, under the threat of an imminent invasion of their country by the Turks. We cannot read these affectionate conversations between the older and the younger Hungarian without thinking of More's letters from the Tower to his daughter Margaret and of the conversations of this kind which More held with her in the Tower—and perhaps also with other members of his family, before his imprisonment. Thus at the outset of the *Dialogue* More has the nephew say:

> We that are likely long to live here in wretchedness have
> need for some comfortable counsel against tribulation to be
> given us by such as you be, good uncle, that have so long
> lived virtuously, and are so learned in the law of God, as
> very few be better in this country here, and have had of
> such things as we now do fear, good experience and assay
> in yourself, as he that hath been taken prisoner in Turkey
> two times in your days and now likely to depart hence ere
> long. . . . But us here shall you leave of your kindred a sort
> [i.e., group] of very comfortless orphans, to all whom your
> good help and counsel and comfort hath long been a great
> stay, not as an uncle unto some, and to some as one further
> of kin, but as though unto us all, you had been a natural
> father.[8]

Yet at the same time More describes the Turkish threat with such exact reference to the historical conditions that we are never allowed to think of this setting as only a device: "Then hath he taken Belgrade, the fortress of this realm. And since hath he destroyed our noble, young goodly king. And now strive there twain for us. Our Lord send the grace that the third dog carry not away the bone from them both" (8). Such allusions to the contemporary situation in Hungary make the setting operate both historically and metaphorically, at one and the same time, with a result that is well stated by John Fowler in the preface to his edition of 1573:

> The invention indeed of the Author seemeth to respect some particular cases, which was of him wonderful wittily devised, applying his whole discourse to that piece of Christendom, to wit, the land of Hungary, which hath been these many years (and yet is) sore persecuted and oppressed by Turks. But under this particular case of Turks' persecution he generally comprehendeth all kinds of afflictions and persecutions, both of body and mind, that may any way be suffered, either by sickness or health, by friend or foe, by wicked and wrongful oppressors, by miscreants and Turks and the very fiends and devils of hell also. And that was done for this intent (as it may well seem), that under this one kind of Turkish persecution the benefit of the book might be the more common to all Christian folk, as the which could justly of none be rejected nor reproved, but if themselves were very Turks too, or worse. [*CW*, 12 : 485–86]

He adds that the book would also be very good for the Turks themselves to read, since they are sometimes taken prisoner by the Christians!

In his universal application of the book, Fowler has found the right key to its spirit and its strategy. It is a book of comfort against all kinds of tribulation, not only against that kind which Thomas More himself is suffering. The treatise seems written at random only if we insist on limiting its concerns to the special situation of More's own treatment at the hands of Henry VIII. More is aware of larger issues than his own fate. He sees his plight as involved in mankind's universal condition. At the same time, as Fowler seems to discern, the generalizing tendency of the treatise serves wittily to disguise its personal implications. "What are you writing there Thomas?" "A book of comfort for those who are sick, or who are tempted by the devil, or who are living in Hungary." So the book escaped suspicion and somehow made its way out of the prison cell.

This general application and disguise is accomplished by means of deliberate garrulity and conscious digression, with the result that the topic of persecution for faith is held in abeyance during the first two books of the treatise, while all the lesser kinds of tribulation are being covered. Then in the final book all strands are drawn together in a subtle, surprising, and powerful way that fulfills the underlying design. Let us see how this design is developed.

Each of the three books has its own peculiar decorum, with a lapse in time before each renewal of the conversation: each book has the effect of a fresh attack upon the universal problem. Book I is composed chiefly of the reassertion of traditional views. The main point is, simply, that tribulation is good for you, if you keep faith. It cures past sins and prevents sins to come. It is a gift of God, the mark of God's favor. But for all his wise utterances here, Uncle Antony finds his nephew hard to convince. Vincent listens respectfully and seems to be taking in the arguments, and yet about three-fifths of the way through the first book he suddenly enters a startling objection:

> But yet, good uncle, though that some do thus, this answereth not full the matter. For we see that the whole church in the common service use divers collects, in which all men pray specially for the princes and prelates, and generally

every man for other, and for himself too, that God would
vouchsafe to send them all perpetual health and prosperity.
And I can see no good man pray God send another sorrow,
nor no such prayers are there put in the priest's portas [i.e.,
breviary] as far as I can hear.

And yet if it were as you say, good uncle, that perpetual
prosperity were to the soul so perilous, and tribulation thereto
so fruitful, then were as me seemeth every man bound of
charity, not only to pray God send their neighbors sorrow,
but also to help thereto themself, and when folk are sick,
not pray God send them health, but when they come to
comfort them they should say, "I am glad, good gossip [i.e.,
friend], that ye be so sick. I pray God keep you long therein."
[48–49]

Antony quells this and other objections by taking the floor
for twelve pages of an unbroken dissertation, closing with a ritual affirmation and "summary comfort" that lists all the bene-
fits of tribulation. One might think that after this resounding
catalogue (see chapter 20) there would not be much more to
say. The effect of a formal conclusion to a formal discourse is
emphasized by the way in which Book I is set forth in twenty
chapters, reasonably divided and of reasonably similar length.
Twenty is a "perfect number," a multiple of ten.

Yet an uneasy feeling persists that the problems of human
suffering cannot be adequately met by the repetition of such
traditional wisdom. The positions set forth by Antony remain
too theoretical, too far removed from actual existence. Such
wisdom is a basis to build upon, no more. Book I is appropri-
ately the shortest of the three.

As the dialogue resumes in Book II, after a lapse of several
days, we are abruptly moved out of the orderly world of theory
and plunged into the chaotic world of every day. Now Antony

and Vincent begin by swapping worldly jests, and Antony at once signals a drastic change in tone and technique when he apologizes in a jocular way for having talked too much the other day, saying that he wished "the last time after you were gone, when I felt myself (to say the truth) even a little weary, that I had not so told you still a long tale alone, but that we had more often interchanged words, and parted the talk between us, with ofter enterparling upon your part, in such manner as learned men use between the persons whom they devise disputing in their feigned dialogues" (82–83). He immediately demonstrates the change in tone by an anecdote, comparing himself with the nun who lectured her brother at length at the convent grate and then berated him for not giving her the benefit of his wisdom. Vincent responds with the "merry tale" concerning the "kinswoman" who loved to talk, which is worth quoting here as an introduction to the more concrete and worldly atmosphere of this entire book:

> Her husband had much pleasure in the manner and behavior of another honest man, and kept him therefore much company, by the reason whereof he was at his mealtime the more oft from home. So happed it on a time that his wife and he together dined or supped with that neighbor of theirs. And then she made a merry quarrel to him, for making her husband so good cheer out at door that she could not have him at home. "Forsooth, mistress," quod he (as he was a dry, merry man), "in my company nothing keepeth him but one. Serve you him with the same, and he will never be from you." "What gay thing may that be?" quoth our cousin then. "Forsooth, mistress," quod he, "your husband loveth well to talk, and when he sitteth with me I let him have all the words." "All the words?" quoth she. "Marry, that am I content he shall have all the words with good will

as he hath ever had, but I speak them all myself, and give them all to him, and for aught that I care for them, so shall he have them still. But otherwise to say that he shall have them all, you shall keep him still rather than he get the half." [84]

While they are thus jesting Antony declares that he will from now on force his nephew to talk half the time. This turns out to be quite a jest in itself, since some of Antony's unbroken dis-quisitions here are in fact even longer than in the first book. Nevertheless, Book II works in quite a different way from Book I. It is thirty-five pages longer,[9] and that extra length, we might say, is filled out with a remarkable array of racy, vivid, collo-quial anecdotes. What we are watching here is a gradual process of adjusting theory to the world as it is, a process that More wittily heralds in the first chapter of Book II by having Vincent ask Antony whether he really meant, in the previous day's con-versation, to rule out all forms of worldly comfort, such as "a merry tale with a friend" or "proper pleasant talking." Antony allows that his theories cannot in fact be so strictly applied, con-sidering that men are as they are: "A man to take now and then some honest worldly mirth, I dare not be so sore as utterly to forbid it" (86). True, we ought to find all our joy and comfort in talking of heaven, but somehow people seem to be easily wea-ried by this topic, as Cassian, he says, shows in one of his *Collations:*

A certain holy father in making of a sermon spake of heaven and of heavenly things so celestially that much of his audi-ence with the sweet sound thereof began to forget all the world and fall asleep. Which when the father beheld, he dissembled their sleeping and suddenly said unto them, "I shall tell you a merry tale." At which word they lift up their heads and hearkened unto that. And after the sleep therewith broken, heard him tell on of heaven again. . . . But thus much of that matter sufficeth for our purpose: that whereas you demand me whether in tribulation men may not sometime refresh themself with worldly mirth and recreation, I can no more say but he that cannot long endure to hold up his head and hear talking of heaven, except he be now and then between (as though heaven were heaviness) refreshed with a foolish merry tale, there is none other remedy, but you must let him have it. Better would I wish it but I cannot help it. [87–88]

Shortly after this Antony becomes so involved in recounting the strange tale of a tertian fever of his, in which he felt hot and cold at once, that he loses his train of thought: "But see now what age is, lo; I have been so long in my tale that I have almost forgotten for what purpose I told it. Oh now I remember, lo" (93).

We are moving ever more clearly and concretely into the world of actuality—the story of the fever includes an allusion to a young woman trained in medicine that almost certainly is a reference to More's adopted daughter, Margaret Clement (92). Now the world's stage opens out suddenly with two brilliant tales involving religious satire. The first is a lengthy narration by Vincent of his recent experiences in Saxony, during the early days of Luther's revolt ("nor Luther was not then wedded yet"). Vincent parodies a Lutheran sermon in words that bring directly home the powerful appeal of the Reformers:

He cried ever out upon them to keep well the laws of
Christ, let go their peevish penance and purpose them to
amend, and seek nothing to salvation but the death of
Christ. "For he is our justice, and he is our Savior, and our

whole satisfaction for all our deadly sins. He did full penance for us all upon his painful cross; he washed us there all
clean with the water of his sweet side, and brought us out
of the devil's danger with his dear precious blood. Leave,
therefore, leave, I beseech you, these inventions of men,
your foolish Lenten fasts and your peevish penance. . . . It
is Christ's death, I tell you, that must save us all, Christ's
death, I tell you yet again, and not our own deeds. Leave
your own fasting, therefore, and lean to Christ alone, good
Christian people, for Christ's dear bitter passion.''

Now so loud and so shrill he cried Christ in their ears,
and so thick he came forth with Christ's bitter passion, and
that so bitterly spoken, with the sweat dropping down his
cheeks, that I marveled not though I saw the poor women
weep. For he made mine hair stand up upon mine head.
And with such preaching were the people so brought in,
that some fell to break the fasts on the fasting days, not
of frailty or of malice first, but almost of devotion, lest
they should take fro Christ the thank of his bitter passion.
[97–98]

Twenty pages later, however, we find the other side of the
picture in the longest and most brilliant tale of the entire treatise,
the five-page beast fable which Antony says he heard from his
old nurse, Mother Maud—More's complete and carefully considered answer to Audley's similar fable about conscience. This
is, among other things, a hilarious piece of anti-clerical satire,
presenting the ass who suffers from an excessively scrupulous
conscience, Father Reynard the fox, the worldly priest who
never worries about fasting, and the wolf, who represents the
utterly unscrupulous and rapacious tendencies of man. When
the wolf comes late to his Lenten confession, on Good Friday,
he explains:

"I durst come no sooner for fear lest you would for my gluttony have given me in penance to fast some part of this Lent."

"Nay, nay," quoth the Father Fox, "I am not so unreasonable, for I fast none of it myself. For I may say to thee, son, here in confession between us twain, it is no commandment of God this fasting, but an invention of man. The priests make folk fast and put them to pain about the moonshine in the water, and do but make folk fools, but they shall make me no such fool, I warrant thee, son. For I eat flesh all this Lent myself, I. Howbeit indeed, because I will not be occasion of slander, I therefore eat it secretly in my chamber out of sight of all such foolish brethren as for their weak scrupulous conscience would wax offended withal. And so would I counsel you to do." [120]

Up to this point, nearly halfway through the second book, we have been within the realm of comical satire, but now, with chapter 15, we move into a darker realm of tales concerning self-destruction. Some of these are savagely comic in their way, such as the opening anecdote of the carpenter's wife who was so fiendish that the devil tempted her to taunt her husband into chopping off her head with his axe: "There were standing other folk by, which had a good sport to hear her chide, but little they looked for this chance till it was done ere they could let [i.e., stop] it. They said they heard her tongue babble in her head and call 'whoreson, whoreson,' twice, after that the head was fro the body" (130).

Although some of the examples are thus touched with grim humor, the larger part of this thirty-five-page discussion of suicide or self-destruction is given over to a serious consideration of the ways by which a man can distinguish the illusions of the devil from the true revelations of God (chapter 16). One may wonder why More devotes so much space to this problem of devilish delusions, with special reference to the temptation of self-destruction. It may be relevant to remember that More was, in his last years, very closely concerned with the question of the truth or falsehood of the revelations allegedly experienced by the Nun of Kent.[10] This question of temptation by demons was a real and pressing issue for More, as we may see from the frequent notation *contra demones* which More wrote in the margins of the book of Psalms which he had with him in the Tower.[11] In this connection it is interesting to note that here in the *Dialogue* More says: "Special verses may there be drawn out of the psalter against the devil's wicked temptations" (159). There is no evidence that More was tempted toward suicide, in the ordinary sense of that word; but in a subtler way the possibility of such a devilish temptation may indeed have been close to More's mind. He dwells at some length upon the case of the "very special, holy man" who was by the devil "brought into such an high spiritual pride" that he became convinced it was God's will that he should destroy himself, "and that thereby should he go straight to heaven" (133–34). More in the Tower had chosen a course that was almost certain to lead to his death. How could he be sure that he was not being assailed by the temptation of spiritual pride? (One thinks of the temptations of Thomas à Becket in T. S. Eliot's play.) But of course the whole section on self-destruction is part of More's effort to make his book useful in comfort against all tribulations for everyman.

Finally, for the last twenty pages of Book II, the discussion turns to a very practical examination of the role of *business* in this world, a term under which More includes the busy search for pleasures of the flesh as well as the search for worldly wealth. In this connection More takes the occasion to explain the necessity of having men of substance in this world, in a passage that sounds like a rebuke to those who would take his *Utopia* as a blueprint for society:

> Men cannot, you wot well, live here in this world, but
> if that some one man provide a mean of living for some
> other many. Every man cannot have a ship of his own, nor
> every man be a merchant without a stock. And these things,
> you wot well, must needs be had. Nor every man cannot
> have a plough by himself. And who might live by the tai-
> lor's craft if no man were able to put a gown to make? Who
> by the masonry, or who could live a carpenter, if no man
> were able to build neither church nor house? Who should
> be the makers of any manner cloth, if there lacked men of
> substance to set sundry sorts awork. . . . surely the rich
> man's substance is the well-spring of the poor man's living.
> [183–84]

It is appropriate that after this reconciliation with the ways of the busy world, Book II should end with the bringing in of a good dinner.

These materials have been reviewed at length in order to stress their rich variety. In Book II nearly every aspect of the world as More knew it is vividly brought before us, in colloquial terms, until we may feel that the turmoil of human existence is in some danger of overwhelming the unity and the direction of the dialogue. This sense of disorder is mirrored in the gradual disintegration of the chapter divisions, so reasonably main-tained in Book I. The first chapter of Book II really belongs with the prologue, since the argument of the book begins only in chapter 2, as Vincent's closing words in chapter 1 indicate: "But now I pray you, good uncle, vouchsafe to proceed in our prin-cipal matter." The summary of chapter 3 shifts to the third per-son, which has not been used before: "He divideth tribulation into three kinds, of which three the last he shortly passeth over." Chapter 4 has no real division in topic from the preceding chapter, and, significantly, it is not provided with any summary—the first example of such an omission. There is no convincing division of topic between chapters 10 and 11, nor between 13 and 14. Toward the end the chapter divisions break down completely, as chapter 16 runs to thirty-seven pages and chapter 17 runs to twenty-two pages—lengths that are especially notable because seven of the earlier chapters have run to only a page or a little more. One has the impression that the whole book has been written without regard to chapter divisions—an impression that continues throughout Book III, where the chapter divisions are, however, more reasonably made, both in topic and in length. One begins to wonder whether the chapter divisions in the last two books are the work of More, or whether they have been imposed by another hand.[12]

In any case, the breakdown in chapter divisions indicates a shift to a different principle of organization. As the danger of disunity threatens, More quietly and firmly brings in the counterforce of reason to control these follies and evils. About a quarter of the way through the second book he brings in the great central text from Psalm 90. This runs like a refrain through the rest of Book II and on through Book III, forming the basis for a sustained set of considerations on the comfort to be found in "the truth of God":

> The prophet saith in the psalm, *Scuto circumdabit te ve-*
> *ritas ejus, non timebis a timore nocturno, a sagitta volante*
> *in die, a negotio perambulante in tenebris, ab incursu et*
> *demonio meridiano:* The truth of God shall compass thee
> about with a pavis; thou shalt not be afeard of the night's
> fear, nor of the arrow flying in the day, nor of the business

walking about in the darknesses, nor of the incursion or
invasion of the devil in the midday. [109]

The intricacy of the discussion that lies ahead is at once shown
here as More repeats, ten times within the space of one page,
that key word *pavis:* the ancient term for a long shield protect-
ing the whole body:

> As God hath faithfully promised to protect and defend those
> that faithfully will dwell in the trust of his help, so will he
> truly perform it. And thee that such one art, will the truth
> of his promise defend, not with a little round buckler that
> scant can cover the head, but with a long large pavis that
> covereth all along the body, made, as holy Saint Bernard
> saith, broad above with the Godhead, and narrow beneath
> with the manhead; so that this pavis is our Savior Christ
> himself.
>
> And yet is not this pavis like other pavises of this world,
> which are not made but in such wise as while it defend-
> eth one part, the man may be wounded upon the tother;
> but this pavis is such that, as the prophet saith, it shall
> round about enclose and compass thee, so that thine enemy
> shall hurt thy soul on no side. For *scuto,* saith he, *circum-*
> *dabit te veritas ejus:* With a pavis shall his truth environ
> and compass thee round about. [109–10]

More then dissects the text, part by part, seeing in it four
kinds of temptations or tribulations, the first three forming the
chief matter of Book II.

1. "*Non timebis a timore nocturno:* Thou shalt not be
   afeard of the fear of the night"—which includes temptations that come from an overly scrupulous conscience,

from the "pusillanimity" of a "timorous mind" (110, 115). This is a fear that in its worst form leads to the temptation of suicide.

2. "*a sagitta volante in die*": from the arrow flying in the day—that is, "the arrow of pride, with which the devil tempteth a man" in prosperity (160).

3. "*negotium perambulans in tenebris* . . . business walking in the darkness"—the business of sensual pleasure and the business of worldly wealth (169).

This whole part of the treatise is pursued in a tantalizing manner of deliberate digression and casual divagation that is foreshadowed in chapter 11, where the basic text is introduced, with Antony saying: "And therefore I shall peradventure, except any further thing fall in our way, with treating of those two verses finish and end all our matter" (109). What falls in our way from here on happens to be about two-thirds of the entire treatise! This consciously ambling and rambling manner is openly maintained by many different asides, such as the explanation that occurs in the middle of the discussion of devilish delusions: "That were somewhat out of our purpose, cousin," says Antony, "sith as I told you before, the man were not then in sorrow and tribulation, whereof our matter speaketh, but in a perilous, merry, mortal temptation; so that if we should, beside our own matter that we have in hand, enter into that too, we might make a lenger work between both, than we could well finish this day. Howbeit, to be short. . . ." (136). Then he continues the admittedly "irrelevant" discussion for a dozen more pages. Similarly, Antony promises to "touch one word or twain of the third temptation . . . and then will we call for our dinner." At this suggestion, Vincent, always concerned for his uncle's health, pleads: "for our Lord's sake, take good heed, uncle, that you forbear not your dinner over-long." "Fear not that, cousin, I warrant you," Antony replies, "for this piece will I make you but short" (169). The piece, of course, runs on for twenty more pages.

The whole of Book II thus serves as a variegated interlude, or as a leisurely prologue, before the main event, which now rushes upon us in the form of the fourth temptation, to which More devotes the whole of Book III, the longest book of all:

> The fourth temptation, cousin, that the prophet speaketh of in the foreremembered psalm . . . is plain, open perse-cution, which is touched in these words, *ab incursu et de-monio meridiano.* And of all his temptations this is the most perilous, the most bitter sharp, and the most rigorous. . . . In this temptation, this plain open persecution for the faith, he cometh even in the very midday, that is to wit, even upon them that have an high light of faith shining in their heart. . . . Therefore saith the prophet that the truth of God shall compass that man round about, that dwelleth in the faithful hope of his help, with a pavis, *ab incursu et demonio meridiano:* from the incursion and the devil of the midday, because this kind of persecution is not a wily temp-tation, but a furious force and a terrible incursion. [204–05]

Here, twelve pages into Book III, is the climax of the mode of repetitious winding by which More pursues his tenacious expli-cation of the basic text; we are now ninety-five pages away from the point at which the text was introduced, and yet the word *pavis* is still ringing, and will continue to ring, as the key-note of the faithful man's belief. In this way the last two books are firmly tied together, while More's explication of the text gradually develops, through its network of repetitions, into an abiding proof that the *pavis* of God is always present to protect the faithful amid the apparent chaos of ordinary life. As the ex-

plication weaves its way among the illustrative, gossipy anecdotes of Book II, we come to feel that the disorder of life is being
brought under the steady control of reason. More's biblical explication, we might say, gradually weaves a net that subdues the
unruly world of anecdote. Yet even this is not enough for full
comfort. The reasoning mind of man may do much, More
seems to say, but the most difficult problem and the richest
comfort remain to be explored.

As the third book opens, the problem is abruptly brought before us: Vincent enters with the news (just received in a letter
from Constantinople) that the Turk is preparing a mighty army
which in all likelihood will be aimed at Hungary. We have returned with a jolt to the threat with which the treatise has begun, a threat whose imminence has gradually receded as More's
discourse has turned to lesser matters. But now the historical
situation, both for the Hungarians and for Thomas More, is
brought in hard upon us, especially when Vincent says:

> I hear at mine ear some of our own here among us, which
> within these few years could no more have borne the name
> of a Turk than the name of the devil, begin now to find little
> fault therein, yea, and some to praise them too, little and
> little as they may, more glad to find faults at every state of
> Christendom: priests, princes, rites, ceremonies, sacraments,
> laws and customs, spiritual, temporal and all. [196]

And there are, he says, even some who "talk as though they
looked for a day when, with a turn unto the Turks' faith, they
should be made masters here of true Christian men's bodies and
owners of all their goods" (199).

Here, then, in this incursion of the mid-day devil, lies the
ultimate temptation by which the soul will stand or fall. In such
a plight the theoretical wisdom of the ages, as presented in Book
I, will not suffice; nor will the toughest reasoning powers of

man, struggling to subdue the world about him, as represented in Book II. In this ultimate danger there is only one recourse: to turn within the self and give the mind over to meditation on the great central facts of the faith: the vanity of worldly things, the facts of death, judgment, hell, and heaven, and above all the great central fact of Christ's Passion.

Thus, in Book III More presents what might be called a treatise on the art of meditation. He advises which topics to seek out and shows by brief examples how to meditate upon these ancient themes: *contemptus mundi*, the Last Things, and the Passion. By such meditation, More argues, it is possible to move with the help of reason into a realm that includes and yet transcends reason: the realm of the affections, the emotions, the love of God.

For all those who fear "bodily pain" and "painful death" in persecution, Uncle Antony recommends "the meditation of [Christ's] great, grievous agony," for, he says, the victim of persecution shall:

> thereupon be so comforted with the secret, inward inspiration of his Holy Spirit, as he was with the personal presence of that angel, that after his agony came and comforted him, that you shall as his true disciple follow him, and with good will without grudge do as he did, and take your cross of pain and passion upon your back, and die for the truth with him, and thereby reign with him crowned in eternal glory.

"And this I say," Antony explains,

> to the intent when a man feeleth such an horror of death in his heart, he should not thereby stand in outrageous fear that he were falling, for many such man standeth for all that fear full fast and finally better abide[th] the brunt, when God is so good unto him as to bring him thereto and

encourage him therein, than doth some other that in the beginning feeleth no fear at all. [252]

The way is thus prepared for More's own meditation on Christ's agony in the Garden of Gethsemane, a work preserved in manuscript as More wrote it, in his own hand.

4

❖ ❖ ❖ ❖ ❖ ❖ ❖ ❖ ❖

De Tristitia
Last Address to the World
and to the Self

The closing chapters of the *Dialogue of Comfort*, with their emphasis upon meditation on the Passion, lead toward the Latin treatise, *De tristitia, tedio, pavore et oratione christi ante captionem eius*, or, in Mary Basset's title, *Of the sorrow, weariness, fear, and prayer of Christ before his taking*—a work which is much more than a continuation of the commentary begun in More's English treatise on the Passion.

It is nevertheless in some sense a continuation, since it begins with the gospel event that follows immediately after the establishment of the Last Supper, the event that closed the English treatise. And the method is somewhat the same: quotation from John Gerson's *Monotessaron*, followed by commentary. Only the short prayers that close each section in the English treatise are omitted. Yet it is distinguished from the English treatise, first, by the difference in language, and second, by the personal application to More himself that gradually emerges from his repeated discussions of Christ's agony as an example and encouragement to the fearful kind of martyr.

Why did More change from English to Latin for his treatment of Christ's agony and capture? More's own capture and the imminent threat of torture and death must, one may conjecture, have motivated the change, for several reasons. First of all, the Latin language made the writing less available to the prying eyes of his keepers, who might be able to read English, but not Latin; here was a certain measure of sanctuary to his inmost thoughts. Second, it was the language of the church for which he was prepared to give his life, the language of the liturgy and the psalms in the prayer book that he kept with him in the Tower, writing in its margins in English one prayer suitable for general use, but writing in Latin his inmost thoughts as he meditated upon the book of psalms. Third, the Latin language enabled him to reach a different audience, just as his Latin version of the history of Richard III had enabled him to reach his peers in the international language of humanism. And finally, the Latin language enabled him to write a treatise more precise, more intense, and more elegant than the English treatise on the Passion. One of the most significant aspects of the Valencia manuscript of the *De Tristitia* is its revelation of the immense amount of revision that More performed upon it, revision extending to the most minute details of grammar and verbal nuance. By studying these revisions we can now understand, in a way never before possible, the humanistic mind of More at work upon the creation of a Latin masterpiece.[1]

It is a moving and appropriate thought that in the somber close of his career More should have sought to communicate with the audience that had admired his *Utopia*. So far as I can judge, the Latin of the *De Tristitia* is in no way inferior in style and effect to the Latin of the *Utopia*. Both treatises form a tribute to More's essential humanism: the earlier work, beloved by Erasmus, which made More famous throughout the humanistic world, and this final work, which remained unpublished for thirty years after More's death. It seems certain that Erasmus never read the *De Tristitia*, but if he had, one suspects that, while admiring its style, he would have disapproved of its tacit defense of More's forthcoming death. Nevertheless, the *De Tristitia* is a document of the most profound humanism, using the letter to hold body and spirit together, using the word to maintain in the mind a vision of Christian unity that spanned all history, all nations, all creatures, all being.

My mention of Erasmus is not incidental to the interpretation of the *De Tristitia* that I now wish to present. For the very title of More's treatise evokes the memory of the work written by Erasmus on the same topic, with a similar title, his *Disputatiuncula de tedio, pauore, tristicia Iesu, instante crucis hora, deque verbis quibus visus est mortem deprecari: Pater, si fieri potest, transeat a me calix iste*—a treatise which grew out of a debate between Erasmus and Colet at Oxford and which was printed no fewer than ten times between 1503 and 1535.[2] The parallel passages cited by Clarence Miller make it clear that More must have had this treatise in mind at several points in his discussion; and he also seems to have used many of Erasmus's notes upon passages of the New Testament.[3] The most striking of these debts (or should one call it a tribute?) occurs in the discussion of irony that arises from the interpretation of the text where Christ for the third time awakens the sleeping apostles, saying: "Why are you sleeping? Sleep on now and take your rest. That is enough. Get up and pray that you may not enter into temptation. Behold, the hour has almost come when the son of man will be betrayed into the hands of sinners. Get up, let us go. Behold, the one who will betray me is near at hand" (*CW*, 14 : 289).

In dealing with the apparent contradiction here, More follows Erasmus against the consensus of all the major fathers of the church, including Augustine.[4] Erasmus insists on the irony, and More joins him in defending the biblical use of their own favorite figure of speech: "Immediately after He had aroused the sleeping apostles for the third time, He undercut them with irony, not indeed that trivial and sportive variety with which idle men of wit are accustomed to amuse themselves, but rather a serious and weighty kind of irony. . . . Notice how," More points out, "He grants permission to sleep in such a way as clearly shows He means to take it away. . . ."

> I am not unaware that some learned and holy men do not allow this interpretation, though they admit that others, equally learned and holy, have found it agreeable. Not that those who do not accept this interpretation are shocked by this sort of irony, as some others are—also pious men to be sure, but not sufficiently versed in the figures of speech

which sacred scripture customarily takes over from common speech. For if they were, they would have found irony in so many other places that they could not have found it offensive here. What could be more pungent or witty than the irony with which the blessed apostle gracefully polishes off the Corinthians?—I mean where he asks pardon because he never burdened any of them with charges and expenses.

"For how have I done any less for you than for the other churches, except this, that I have never been a burden to you? Pardon me for this injustice." What could be more forceful or biting than the irony with which God's prophet ridiculed the prophets of Baal as they called upon the deaf statue of their god: "Call louder," he said, "for your god is asleep or perhaps has gone somewhere on a trip." I have taken this occasion to bring up these instances in passing, because some readers, out of a certain pious simplicity, refuse to accept in sacred scripture (or at least do not notice there) these universally used forms of speech, and by neglecting the figures of speech they very often miss the real sense of scripture. [CW, 14 : 289, 293–97]

After this typically humanistic stress on the interpretation of "forms of speech" More then comes to the most difficult problem, for his favorite father of the church has taken a quite different view: "Now concerning this passage St. Augustine says that he finds the interpretation I have given to be not unacceptable but also not necessary. He claims that the plain meaning without any figure is adequate." He then explains Augustine's argument in detail, concluding with what seems to be great admiration: "Subtle indeed this reasoning of the most blessed Augustine, as he always is"; but More goes on in his bland way to disagree: "but I imagine that those of the opposite persuasion do not find it at all likely that, after Christ had already re-

proached them twice for sleeping when His capture was imminent, and after He had just rebuked them sternly by saying
'Why are you sleeping?' He should then have granted them
time to sleep, especially at the very time when the danger which
was the reason they ought not to have slept before, was now
pounding on the door, as they say." Still, More adds, I don't
really mean to stress any one point of view! I simply offer an
open choice: "But now that I have presented both interpreta-
tions, everyone is free to choose whichever he likes. My purpose has been merely to recount both of them; it is not for such
a nobody as me to render a decision like an official arbitrator"
(*CW*, 14 : 297, 301–03).

A few lines later we find More quoting Horace, while urging
people to follow Christ's injunction, "Get up and pray": "Since
this sort of remedy was handed down by our Savior Himself, I
heartily wish that we would occasionally be willing to try it out
at the dead of night. For here we would discover not only that
well begun is half done (as Horace says) but that once begun is
all done."[5] This quotation may remind us that, whereas the
classics play no part in the English treatise on the Passion, a
considerable number of overt allusions to the classics are scat-
tered throughout this Latin treatise, along with numerous tacit
echoes of familiar classical phrases from Vergil, Cicero, Juvenal,
Terence, and many others,[6] all reminding us of More's similar
practice in his *Ad Lutherum* and his humanistic letters. Some
of these allusions are couched in a familiar way that indicates
the presence of the audience assumed by the language—an audience humanistically educated, though not, of course, always
to the level of an Erasmus. Thus, we have an allusion to Alex-
ander as "the debauched Macedonian," a quotation from Terence
identified only as "that saying of the comic poet," and a quotation from Juvenal identified by the words, "as the satirist says."
Along with these we have overt allusions to Vergil, the Stoics,

and "the cynic sect" (reminding us that More, some thirty years before, had made a Latin version of Lucian's dialogue "The Cynic").[7] This classical coloring is far from dominant, but its presence, intermingled with the dominant biblical texture, is another sure indication of the humanist at work.

But the best indication of the educated audience More is addressing lies in his constant care for elegant, precise, and powerful phrasing in the humanistic mode. One of the best examples of this style is found in the imaginative extension that More creates to explain the significance of Christ's address to Peter: "Simon, are you sleeping"—"et tu Simon dormis?" "et tu . . ."

> I always made much of you Simon, and yet Simon are you sleeping? I paid you many high honors, and yet Simon are you sleeping? A few moments ago you boasted that you would die with me, and now Simon are you sleeping? Now I am pursued to the death by the Jews and the gentiles and by one worse than either of them, Judas, and Simon are you sleeping? Indeed, Satan is busily seeking to sift all of you like wheat, and Simon are you sleeping? What can I expect from the others, when, in such great and pressing danger, not only to me but also to all of you, I find that you Simon, even you are sleeping? [CW, 14 : 165–67]

This whole passage has emerged after a great deal of revision, mainly aimed at giving a resounding length and strength to the final portion.

In other places More gives particular attention to the rhetorical emphasis and compactness gained by the use of assonance. For example, in the long climactic speech of Christ on the theme "This is your hour and the power of darkness," More creates the following crescendo: "This is your short hour. This is that mad and ungovernable power which brings you armed to take an unarmed man, which brings the fierce against the gentle, criminals against an innocent man, a traitor against his lord, puny mortals against God." ("Hec est breuis hora uestra. Hec est amens et impotens potestas tenebrarum / qua nunc armati comprehendetis inermem / truculenti mitem / nocentes innocuum / proditor dominum / homunciones deum"; *CW*, 14 : 541–43).

More is creating, then, his last work in the best Latin style that he can achieve, revising, adding, filling in the margins with hundreds of revised or added passages, canceling three whole pages, or adding two whole pages to a gathering. One thinks of George Herbert's words, "My God must have my best." But along with this Herbertian desire to appear in the presence of God "well drest" there lies another meaning, a subtle irony, and a poignant appeal.

The closest analogy to More's two treatises on the Passion is found in a popular work of the late Middle Ages, the *Vita Christi* of Ludolph the Carthusian, which follows the traditional threefold structure for each biblical event: reading, meditation, and prayer—or rather, scriptural quotation, exposition, and prayer.[8] In both the English and the Latin treatise on the Passion by More, one cannot escape an awareness of the continuity of tradition from such treatises of the late Middle Ages into More's own writing. But in each of More's treatises a clear difference is also quickly evident in More's manner of writing and thinking. His manner is free from scholastic divisions and disquisitions; his whole aim is to draw the spiritual, the moral meaning from the letter; and this is done, in the English treatise, in a way that everyone who can read or hear will understand.

This manner continues in the Latin treatise, available to all those who know Latin, not simply addressed to the learned humanist. Thus, his disquisition on avoiding distractions in prayer is couched in witty, earthy words that would appeal to any person who could handle the language at all.[9] Addresses to the reader continue, as in the English treatise, and matters are explained that would need no such explanation for those well versed in theology and in the art of scriptural interpretation. Such is the outward manner of address: all is objective, public; no issues personal, specially related to the writer, are conceded. And yet for everyone who reads with the knowledge of this writer's situation, the defense of the faint-hearted, fearful kind of martyr takes on a poignant personal application that cannot and should not be avoided. One hears in these passages the voice of More pleading with his fellow humanists to understand his reasons for following the way that he has chosen, so different from the way of Erasmus. He is still the same man who wrote *Utopia* and translated Lucian; he still loves the ironies and the elegant Latin that they all sought to achieve. Here is no throwback to the days of the schoolmen, not at all. The work may at first look like an inheritance from Ludolph the Carthusian and similar writers of the late Middle Ages, but the Latin speaks otherwise. It is the Latin of the humanist, seeking for the moral interpretation that the humanist, and above all Erasmus, sought. More writes in a style that Erasmus would approve, even as More explains the different fate that he has chosen, and how he has chosen to meet it, with caution, using whatever laws or means can honorably be used, without breach of faith, to escape or delay the execution which he must know is now inevitable. But it is not for him to step out and boldly demand his fate. The better way, the safer way, is to be fearful, to ask, after Christ's example, that the cup be withdrawn, if God so wills.

One must admire the subtle ironies by which More manages to convey an impression that perhaps the cautious, fearful martyrs are, in some respects, to be admired more than the bold ones:

At this point, if someone should again bring up those
martyrs who freely and eagerly exposed themselves to death
because of their faith in Christ, and if he should offer his
opinion that they are especially worthy of the laurels of
triumph because with a joy that left no room for sorrow
they betrayed no trace of sadness, no sign of fear, I am
perfectly willing to go along with him on that point, so long
as he does not go so far as to deny the triumph of those
who do not rush forth of their own accord but who nevertheless do not hang back or withdraw once they have been
seized, but rather go on in spite of their fearful anxiety and
face the terrible prospect out of love for Christ. [*CW*,
14 : 237–39]

But More is quick to insist that he does not wish to take away
any glory from these bold martyrs: "Now if anyone should argue that the eager martyrs receive a greater share of glory than
the others, I have no objection—he can have the argument all
to himself [per me licebit secum contendat solus]. For I rest con-
tent with the fact that in heaven neither sort of martyr will lack
a glory so great that while they were alive their eyes never saw
the like. . . ."

Besides, just who outranks whom in the glory assigned
by God in heaven is not, I think, quite crystal-clear to us,
groping as we are in the darkness of our mortality.
For, though I grant that God loves a cheerful giver, still I
have no doubt that He loved Tobias, and holy Job too. Now
it is true that both of them bore their calamities bravely and
patiently, but neither of them, so far as I know, was exactly
jumping with joy or clapping his hands out of happiness.
To expose one's self to death for Christ's sake when the
case clearly demands it or when God gives a secret prompt-

ing to do so, this, I do not deny, is a deed of preeminent
virtue. But otherwise I do not think it very safe to do so,
and among those who willingly suffered for Christ we find
outstanding figures who were very much afraid, who were
deeply distressed, who even withdrew from death more than
once before they finally faced it bravely. [*CW*, 14 : 239–43]

"Certainly," More at once explains, "I do not mean to derogate
from God's power to inspire martyrs," but he then goes on to
deliver a rather back-handed sort of praise for the martyr whose
mind is filled with joy:

> Since we often see it happen that some men do not feel
> wounds inflicted in battle until their awareness, which had
> been displaced by strong feeling, returns to them and they
> notice the injury, certainly there is no reason why I should
> doubt that a mind exulting in the high hopes of approaching
> glory can be so rapt and transported beyond itself that it
> neither fears death nor feels torments.
>
> But still, even if God did give someone this gift, I would
> certainly be inclined to call it an unearned felicity or the
> recompense of past virtue, but not the measure of future
> reward in heaven. [*CW*, 14 : 243–45]

More then delivers an even more direct qualification of the
virtues of the bold martyr: "Besides," he asks, "is it not possible that God in His goodness removes fear from some persons
not because He approves of or intends to reward their boldness,
but rather because He is aware of their weakness and knows
that they would not be equal to facing fear." He agrees, of
course, that "those who eagerly suffer death encourage others
by their example," but he adds, in a long rhetorical sentence
that rises to a resounding climax, the following alternative:

But on the other hand, since almost all of us are fearful in
the face of death, who can know how many have also been
helped by those whom we see face death with fear and trem-
bling but whom we also observe as they break bravely through
the hindrances blocking their path, the obstacles barring
their way with barriers harder than steel, that is, their own
weariness, fear, and anguish, and by bursting these iron
bars and triumphing over death take heaven by storm?
[CW, 14 : 243–47]

With such examples of the fearful martyr before us, he asks,
"will not weaklings who are, like them, cowardly and afraid
take heart so as not to yield under the stress of persecution even
though they feel great sadness welling up within them, and fear
and weariness and horror at the prospect of a ghastly death?"
Nevertheless, More continues to insist, he is not arguing that
one kind of martyr is better than another: "The whole drift of
the present discussion finally comes to this: we should admire
both kinds of most holy martyrs, we should venerate both
kinds, praise God for both, we should imitate both when the
situation demands it, each according to his own capacity and according to the grace God gives to each." Yet the argument is
still not settled. He has one more "but" to add: still another
warning against excessive boldness:

But the person who is conscious of his own eagerness
needs not so much encouragement to be daring as perhaps a
reminder to be afraid lest his presumption, like Peter's, lead
to a sudden relapse and fall. But if a person feels anxious,
heavy-hearted, fearful, certainly he ought to be comforted
and encouraged to take heart. For both sorts of martyrs this
anguish of Christ is most salutary: it keeps the one from
being over-exultant and makes the other be of good hope
when his spirit is crestfallen and downcast. [CW, 14 : 247–51]

The sinuous, subtle, shifting argument seems quite Erasmian in its movement, its ironic undertones, its bland assertions of an equable position, while all the time leaning toward one side of the argument.

Finally, deepest of all, one may discern in the *De Tristitia* another indispensable component of the best in Renaissance, humanist works of art: the presence of the individual self, the presence of the artist as a person and a personality. So Milton and Spenser include the voice of the bard within their poems, as Ariosto and Camoens had done before. So Raphael includes the portraits of his friends in his vision of the classical philosophers. So More includes his friends and a version of himself, by name, in his great *Utopia*. And so here, in his final writing, the voice of the individual self is not repressed. It is there, constantly speaking within the framework, the guise or disguise, of a traditional objective commentary on the gospel. The homely moralizing found in some places, so ordinary, so conventional—does this not have an effect of disguising the underlying voice of the subtle humanist? Yet that voice clearly emerges from time to time, saying "I have sometimes asked myself this question," or "Here, then, is how I would imagine it." Such emergence of the speaking self serves to remind us that the mode of the first person speaking is actually dominant in the treatise. "Ego" and "Mihi" are often prominently placed, as if to say, to *me* all this is being spoken, as well as to you, my faithful reader. This central voice draws all together in a powerful finale.

Just as More's English treatise on the Passion had reached a climax and conclusion in the three lectures on the sacrament of the Eucharist, so here his Latin treatise reaches its climax and conclusion in three carefully charted sections, marked for special attention by the device of subheads, not used elsewhere in the treatise. This finale was first given a general title, "De amputata Malchi auricula apostolorum fuga et captione christi"

(*CW*, 14 : 466), thus setting off the final portion in the way that, perhaps, the final portion of the English treatise on the Passion was set off by a subhead: "To receive the blessed body of our Lord, sacramentally and virtually both." [10] But later More decided to subdivide his conclusion to the *De Tristitia* and to provide separate headings for the last two sections: "De fuga disciplorum" and, lastly, "De christi captione" (*CW*, 14 : 558, 618). He therefore crossed out the last two phrases in the original heading.

The section on "the severing of Malchus' ear" is by far the longest of the three final sections, which show a striking diminuendo, dropping from forty-six pages to thirty, and then to four. The first section is not only the longest; it is also the most highly wrought in its rhetoric. For here is the fearful moment of truth; what Christ has foretold is now "happening before their very eyes," bringing mental confusion and turmoil:

> When the apostles saw what was about to happen, their
> minds were overwhelmed by a sudden welter of different
> feelings: anxiety for their Lord whom they loved, fear for
> their own safety, and finally shame for that high-sounding
> promise of theirs that they would all rather die than fail
> their master. Thus their impulses were divided between
> conflicting feelings. Their love of their master urged them
> not to flee; their fear for themselves, not to remain. Fear of
> death impelled them to run away; shame for their promise,
> to stand fast. [*CW*, 14 : 467–69]

In this confusion Peter tries the wrong way of violence, and the apostles must learn the better way of suffering. For it is now clear that the cup will not be taken away. Christ must stand forth and face his enemies with those bold and bitter words of acceptance: "This is your hour and the power of darkness." Upon this text More creates the climactic passage of this entire treatise: the imagined words of Christ to the assembled host, words that represent the traditional inward speaking of Christ to the faithful soul, as in the *Imitation of Christ* (*CW*, 14:537–57). But how different in style and manner from the simple speaking heard in the treatise of Thomas à Kempis! For Thomas More writes here nothing less than a small classical oration, a Phillipic, or a Catilinian oration, exactly the kind of formal speech that he had long ago imagined for his speakers in the humanistic history of Richard III. It flows along with unbroken power, not extensively revised. More is sure now, and he writes securely; he shows none of the insecurity and hesitancy that marked his very heavily revised sections on the fearful martyr. Twining and intertwining throughout the oration, the basic text moves through a dozen variations:

> But this hour and this power of darkness are not only given to you now against me, but such an hour and such a brief power of darkness will also be given to other governors and other caesars against other disciples of mine. . . . And they will stand against the snares of the devil, that is, against the soft speeches he will place on the lips of their persecutors to cajole them into leaving the way of truth. The open assaults of Satan they will also resist on the evil day. . . . For the span of time allotted to your wanton arrogance is not endless but has been shortened to the span of a brief hour for the sake of the elect, that they might not be tried beyond their strength. And so this hour of yours and this power of darkness are not long-lasting and enduring but quite as brief as the present moment to which they are limited, an instant of time always caught between a past that is gone and a future that has not arrived. Therefore, lest you should lose any of this hour of yours which is so short, proceed immediately to use it for your own evil pur-

poses. Since you seek to destroy me, be quick about it, arrest me without delay, but let these men go their way. [*CW*, 14 : 543–57]

Then comes the ultimate, terrible irony, as More writes the next verse of the gospel at the very close of this triumphant speech: "Then all the disciples abandoned Him and fled."

The following section drops down to a different mode, quiet, filled with the personal voice in a degree not evidenced earlier: "I have sometimes asked myself this question: when Christ left off praying and returned to the apostles only to find them sleeping, did He go to both groups or only to those He had brought farther along and placed nearest to Him? But when I consider these words of the evangelist, 'All of them abandoned Him and fled,' I no longer have any doubt that it was all of them who fell asleep" (*CW*, 14 : 561–63). More does not dwell long, however, upon the flight of the disciples, which Christ both permitted and encouraged. He turns instead to ponder at great length the meaning of the presence of that "certain young man" who wore "only a linen cloth wrapped about his naked body," and who, when grasped by the crowd, threw off this cloth and "fled from them naked."

"Just who this young man was has never been determined with certainty," says More, and he then runs through all the possibilities in a quiet, detached, reasonable, witty, and amused tone that shows a mind wholly in control of every passion. Here is More the man speaking openly to us, using the first person in a relaxed, informal, and friendly way. More sides with those who think the young man "was not one of the apostles at all but one of the servants in the household where Christ had celebrated the Passover that night." "And certainly," More continues, "I myself find this opinion easier to accept. Apart from the fact that I find it unlikely for an apostle to be wearing nothing but a linen cloth, and even that so loosely fastened that it could be quickly thrown off, I am inclined to this opinion first of all by the sequence of historical events and then by the very words of the account." He goes on to note that among those who would identify the young man as an apostle, John is the favorite candidate. But, he adds, these people "are faced with a slight hitch in their argument—namely, the fact that he threw off the linen cloth and fled naked. For this seems to conflict with what follows—namely, that John entered the courtyard of the high priest, that he brought Peter in . . . that he followed Christ all the way to the place of the crucifixion. . . ." More adds drily, "Now there can be no doubt that at all these times and in all these places John was wearing clothes. For he was a disciple of Christ, not of the cynic sect. . . . This difficulty they try to explain away by saying that he went somewhere else in the meantime and put on other clothes—a point I will not dispute, but it hardly seems likely to me, especially when I see in this passage that he continuously followed after Christ with Peter. . . ." More then continues to dispute the point with other evidence, finally coming to his own interpretation, where we find the basic reason for More's preference: "Here, then, is how I would imagine it. This young man, who had previously been excited by Christ's fame and who now saw Him in person as he was bringing in food to Christ and His disciples reclining at table [in good Roman fashion, we might note], was touched by a secret breath of the spirit and felt the moving force [the virtue, we might say] of charity. Then, impelled to pursue a life of true devotion, he followed Christ when He left after dinner and continued to follow Him, at a little distance, perhaps, from the apostles but still with them" [*CW*, 14 : 565–79].

Here is the true, the *virtual* effect of devout attendance at the Last Supper; the young man is the first, beyond the band of the apostles, to feel the effects of the sacrament. He is a figure for every devout soul, a servant of the Lord. And he becomes a figure for the fate of Thomas More in the allegory that More presents as his final interpretation of this event, an interpretation for which no precedent has been found. It is More's very own, the closest to his heart. The young man becomes a figure of the soul casting off the body to escape the earth and reach eternity:

> But, as I was saying, to avoid falling into grave sin we must throw off not merely a cloak or gown or shirt or any other such garment of the body but even the garment of the soul, the body itself. For if we strive to save the body by sin, we destroy it and we also lose the soul. But if we patiently endure the loss of the body for the love of God, then, just as the snake sloughs off its old skin (called, I think, its "senecta") by rubbing it against thorns and thistles, and leaving it behind in the thick hedges comes forth young and shining, so too those of us who follow Christ's advice and become wise as serpents will leave behind on earth our old bodies, rubbed off like a snake's old skin among the thorns of tribulation suffered for the love of God, and will quickly be carried up to heaven, shining and young and never more to feel the effects of old age. [CW, 14:615–17]

After this, perhaps we should not be surprised at the briefness of the final section, "De christi captione." There is little for More to add, except, in true scholarly fashion, to determine the exact time when Christ was captured, to acknowledge the chief source used, and to sum up the evidence of the immense power that Christ possessed, but, in his charity, refused to use. Here, as More reaches his conclusion, he rolls off his longest series of rhetorical parallels and the most emphatic of all his classically suspended sentences. I have quoted Mary Basset's translation of this passage at the end of chapter 3, but now it seems essential to hear the Latin, with all its humanistic flourishes:

post osculo dato regressum ad cohortem et Iudeos Iudam / post prostratam christi sola voce cohortem / post amputatam sanatamque rursus serui summi sacerdotis auriculam / post cohibitos ne pugnarent reliquos / post increptium qui pugnarat petrum / post compellatos iterum qui tum aderant magistratus iudeorum denunciatamque quod ante non poterant capiendi tum concessam facultatem / post apostolos omnes elapsos fuga / post adolescentem qui quamquam captus teneri non potuit alacri nuditate seruatum / tum demum primum manus iniectas in Iesum. [*CW*, 14:623–25]

Notes

Chapter 1: The Search for the Inner Man

This essay is based upon the R. W. Chambers Memorial Lecture delivered at University College, London, in February 1987, with major revisions and additions derived from a lecture delivered at Yale University in March 1988 as part of a symposium on More.

1 G. R. Elton, "Thomas More, Councillor," in *St. Thomas More: Action and Contemplation*, ed. R. S. Sylvester (New Haven: Yale University Press, 1972), pp. 87–122; included in Elton, *Studies in Tudor and Stuart Politics and Government*, 2 vols. (Cambridge: Cambridge University Press, 1974), I, 129–54; "The Real Thomas More?" in *Reformation Principle and Practice*, ed. Peter Newman Brooks (London: Scolar Press, 1980), pp. 23–31; Richard Marius, *Thomas More* (New York: Knopf, 1984).

2 *New York Times*, 4 January 1987, Section H, p. 5.

3 *The Yale Edition of The Complete Works of St. Thomas More* (New Haven: Yale University Press, 1963—), 8 : 590. (Referred to hereafter as *CW*.) The passage is cited by Marius, p. 406.

4 More is here explaining why he "advised and helped" to have Philips sent to the Tower instead of to the bishop's prison; it was, he says, because he feared that Philips might commit suicide in the bishop's prison and thus bring about another anti-clerical uproar such as attended the death of Richard Hunne, which More believed to be a suicide; see *CW*, 9 : 126–27.

5 G. R. Elton, *Reform and Reformation* (London: Arnold, 1977), pp. 191–92. For a detailed account of the executions for treason after More's departure from office and Cromwell's assumption of power (1532–1540), see Elton, *Policy and Police: The Enforcement of the Reformation in the Age of Thomas Cromwell* (Cambridge: Cambridge University Press, 1972), especially pp. 383–400.

6 J. A. Guy, *The Public Career of Sir Thomas More* (New Haven: Yale University Press, 1980), pp. 166–67.

7 See *Holbein and the Court of Henry VIII* (Catalogue of an Exhibi-

tion in The Queen's Gallery, Buckingham Palace, 1978), p. 28, item 2. See also K. T. Parker, *The Drawings of Hans Holbein in the Collection of His Majesty the King at Windsor Castle*, second ed. (Oxford and London: Phaidon Press, 1945), p. 36, item 2.

8 See the discussion of this painting in Stanley Morison, *The Likeness of Thomas More* (New York: Fordham University Press, 1963), pp. 18–25. For further illustrations and details of the lettering on the books see M. W. Brockwell, *Catalogue of the Pictures at Nostell Priory* (1913), pp. 79 ff.

9 Thomas More, *Selected Letters*, ed. Elizabeth Frances Rogers (New Haven: Yale University Press, 1961), pp. 146–47.

10 See Elton, "The Real Thomas More?"; Marius, pp. xxi–xxiii and chapter 3, "Priesthood or Marriage."

11 See his treatise on the "last things", dated "around" the year 1522 in Rastell's edition of More's *Works*, 1557.

12 Nicholas Harpsfield, *The Life and Death of Sr Thomas Moore*, ed. Elsie Vaughan Hitchcock (London: Early English Text Society, Oxford University Press, 1932), p. 12.

13 Harpsfield is wrong with regard to Thomas Lupset here; at this time More was actually learning Greek from Thomas Linacre.

14 Thomas Stapleton, in the latest of the three early lives of More, is responsible for much of the emphasis upon More's desire to become a monk and for his alleged regret about his decision to marry. After asserting that "he was far more zealous to become a saint than a scholar," and stressing his ascetic practices, Stapleton adds: "For the religious state he had an ardent desire, and thought for a time of becoming a Franciscan. But as he feared, even with the help of his practices of penance, that he would not be able to conquer the temptations of the flesh that come to a man in the vigour and ardour of his youth, he made up his mind to marry. Of this he would often speak in after life with great sorrow and regret, for he used to say that it was much easier to be chaste in the single than in the married state." *The Life and Illustrious Martyrdom of Sir Thomas More*, trans. Philip E. Hallett (London: Burns Oates, 1928), pp. 9–10. But, as Hallett notes, Stapleton's "primary object was not to write a history, but rather a devotional work for the edification of his readers" (ix). The life is the third of three saints' lives in his Latin work *Tres Thomae* (1588), the other saints being Thomas the Apostle and Thomas à Becket.

15 Clarence Miller suggests: "All More is saying is that if he didn't have a wife and children, he would have retired long since (that is, after leaving the chancellorship) to some small room to pray, meditate, and write."

16 See the famous letter of Erasmus to Ulrich von Hutten, 23 July 1519. The passage concerning More's decision to marry needs close examination: "Interim et ad pietatis studium totum animum appulit, vigiliis, ieiuniis, precationibus aliisque consimilibus progymnasmatis sacerdotium meditans. . . . Neque quicquam obstabat quo minus sese huic vitae generi addiceret, nisi quod vxoris desyderium non posset excutere. Maluit igitur maritus esse castus quam sacerdos impurus." He performed various spiritual exercises, "considering the priesthood." "Nothing stood in the way of giving himself to this kind of life, except that he was not able to shake off his desire for a wife. Therefore he chose to be a chaste husband rather than an impure priest." Erasmus provides the witty interpretation in the last sentence. See Erasmus, *Opus Epistolarum*, ed. P. S. Allen et al. 12 vols. (Oxford: Clarendon Press, 1906–58), IV, 17–18.

17 Elton, *Studies in Tudor and Stuart Politics and Government*, I, 149.

18 Marius, p. 280.

19 John Milton, *Apology*, in *Complete Prose Works*, ed. Don M. Wolfe et al., 8 vols. (New Haven: Yale University Press, 1953–82), I, 899–903.

20 Milton, Preface to *Animadversions*, *Complete Prose Works*, I, 662–64.

21 See Marius, p. 289: "Unpleasant as it is, the *Responsio ad Lutherum* brings us as close to the real Thomas More as anything else he wrote until that time. Here he had the freedom to be himself, unfettered by the formal demands art made in his *History of King Richard III* or *Utopia*. Here was where he could pour out the deepest passions of his soul in the belief that those passions coincided exactly with the will of God." See also pp. 338–39, where Marius speaks of the "parade of English polemical works from More's pen that for all their ferocity and dreary dullness still offer the most significant literary monument we have to his mind and heart." One result of this view in the Marius biography is the decision to treat More's account of the Richard Hunne case in the

context of More's early career—that is, in 1514–15, when the Hunne case caused anti-clerical disturbances. More's satirical account of the witnesses in the case (*CW*, 6 : 316–30) dates from 1529, when he wrote it as part of his *Dialogue Concerning Heresies:* the satire ridicules the flimsy grounds of gossip that can lead to anti-clerical uproar. The passage tells us much about More's satirical wit as a polemicist; it tells us little, in my view, about his heart, and certainly nothing about his early years.

22 See Marius, p. 339.

23 Stephen Greenblatt, *Renaissance Self-Fashioning* (Chicago: University of Chicago Press, 1980), p. 73. For an account of "a pattern of progressive deterioration" in More's controversial writings, see Alistair Fox, *Thomas More: History and Providence* (New Haven: Yale University Press, 1983), Part 2.

24 I am not convinced that More's frequent repetition of this charge shows any peculiar sexual obsession; see chapter 2.

25 See, for example, the passage (*CW*, 8 : 403–04) where Tyndale gives a rousing statement of the central principle of Reformation doctrine, justification by faith, and More's answer seems to falter and ramble.

26 See Alistair Fox, pp. 187–98, and John Guy's introduction to More's *Debellation*, *CW*, 10 : xvii–xxviii.

27 My pagination is given according to the edition of the *Apology* in *CW*, 9.

28 *Utopia*, ed. Edward Surtz, S. J., and J. H. Hexter (New Haven: Yale University Press, 1965), *CW*, 4 : 99–103.

Chapter 2: The Order of the Heart

1 *The Apology*, ed. J. B. Trapp (New Haven: Yale University Press, 1979), *CW*, 9 : 3; I am indebted to the fine Introduction.

2 *The Confutation of Tyndale's Answer*, ed. Louis A. Schuster, Richard C. Marius, James P. Lusardi, and Richard J. Schoeck (New Haven: Yale University Press, 1973), *CW*, 8.

3 Blaise Pascal, *Pensées*, ed. M. Léon Brunschvicg, 5th ed. (Paris: Hachette, 1909); trans. W. P. Trotter (New York: Dutton, 1958). See also Jacques Maritain, "St. Augustine and St. Thomas Aqui-

nas," in *A Monument to Saint Augustine* (London: Sheed and Ward, 1930).

4 *The Answer to a Poisoned Book*, ed. Stephen Merriam Foley and Clarence H. Miller (New Haven: Yale University Press, 1985), *CW*, 11 : lxxi.

5 See Germain Marc'hadour, *Thomas More et la Bible* (Paris: J. Vrin, 1969), pp. 311–12.

6 *Treatise on the Passion*, ed. Garry E. Haupt (New Haven: Yale University Press, 1976), *CW*, 13 : 64.

7 See introduction to *A Dialogue of Comfort*, ed. Louis L. Martz and Frank Manley (New Haven: Yale University Press, 1976), *CW*, 12 : lxxix–lxxxiii.

8 *De Tristitia Christi*, ed. and trans. Clarence H. Miller (New Haven: Yale University Press, 1976), *CW*, 14 : 43–47.

9 See *CW*, 14 : 1060, note on 619/1.

Chapter 3: Last Letters and *A Dialogue of Comfort*

1 *Selected Letters*, pp. 217–23.

2 *Selected Letters*, pp. 228–34.

3 *The Correspondence of Sir Thomas More*, ed. Elizabeth Frances Rogers (Princeton, N.J.: Princeton University Press, 1947), pp. 514–32.

4 *Correspondence*, pp. 512–13.

5 More's *Works* (1557), sig. YY₁v; *Correspondence*, p. 514 (with the reading "himself" instead of "herself").

6 *CW*, 12 : 114–20.

7 Harpsfield, p. 134. His statement derives from More's statement that a very short letter to Margaret has been "written with a coal" and from Rastell's notes saying that another very short letter, as well as his last (longer) letter, were also written "with a coal" (*Correspondence*, pp. 507, 511, 563).

8 Quotations are taken from the modernized edition: *A Dialogue of Comfort*, ed. Frank Manley (New Haven: Yale University Press, 1977); a volume in the *Selected Works* based upon *CW*, 12.

9 As measured by the pagination in *CW*, 12.

10 See R. W. Chambers, *Thomas More* (London: Cape, 1935), pp.

294–300, and J. Duncan M. Derrett, "Sir Thomas More and the Nun of Kent," *Moreana*, 15–16 (1967), pp. 267–84.

11 *Thomas More's Prayer Book*, ed. L. L. Martz and R. S. Sylvester (New Haven: Yale University Press, 1969), pp. 27, 29, 31, 32, 50, 59, 66, 67, 100, 101, 106, 111, 115.

12 This impression is borne out by the hitherto unknown manuscript of the *Dialogue of Comfort* recently acquired by the Osborn Collection in the Beinecke Library of Yale University; here the scribe has left blank spaces for the chapter numbers in the latter part of Book II, while retaining the headings. It would appear that in the manuscript from which he is copying the division into chapters was tentative or incomplete.

Chapter 4: Last Address to the World and to the Self

1 See Clarence Miller's discussion of style in *CW*, 14 : 745–76 and his detailed account of the revisions in *CW*, 14 : 789–999. I am indebted in this chapter to his illuminating introduction and commentary in this volume of the *Complete Works*.

2 See *CW*, 14 : 1003 and Giovanni Santinello, "Thomas More's *Expositio Passionis*," in *Essential Articles for the Study of Thomas More*, ed. R. S. Sylvester and G. P. Marc'hadour (Hamden, Conn.: Archon Books, 1977), pp. 455–61.

3 For parallel passages between *De Tristitia* and these works of Erasmus, see *CW*, 14, notes to 41/5–43/4, 51/3–4, 55/1, 59/2–4, 83/1–2, 85/1–6, 87/5–89/1, 91/7–93/1, 95/1–4, 101/1–7, 229/2–4, 235/7–237/2, 277/4–279/4, 289/11–291/11, 293/10–295/4, 479/3–4, 565/7–567/6, 629/8–9.

4 See *CW*, 14 : 1030–31, Santinello, p. 456.

5 *CW*, 14 : 303: "quod ut ait horatius Dimimium facti qui cepit habet." From Horace's Epistles, I, ii. 40.

6 See, for example, the following passages in *CW*, 14 with corresponding notes: 81/4, 223/7–8, 267/3–4, 339/9, 403/2–3, 427/1–2, 525/1,6, 527/8, 559/4–6, 599/4.

7 See *CW*, 14 : 147/3, 349/1–3, 473/5–6, 329/6–7, 243/6–8, 573/2.

8 See Garry Haupt's discussion in *CW*, 13 : xcv–c.

9 *CW*, 14 : 117–43.

10 See *CW*, 12 : lxxix–lxxxiii and *CW*, 14 : 741 *n*.

Index